Kokomo-Howard County PUBLIC LIBRARY

220 North Union St.
Kokomo, Indiana 46901-4614
(765) 457-3242
www.KHCPL.org

W9-BNF-969

The Power of Slow

Also by Christine Louise Hohlbaum

S.A.H.M. I Am

Diary of a Mother

The Power of Slow

101 Ways to Save Time in Our 24/7 World

Christine Louise Hohlbaum

St. Martin's Press ≋ New York

www.stmartins.com

Book design by Ruth Lee-Mui

Library of Congress Cataloging-in-Publication Data

Hohlbaum, Christine Louise.
  The power of slow : 101 ways to save time in our 24/7 world / Christine Louise Hohlbaum. — 1st ed.
      p. cm.
  Includes bibliographical references.
  ISBN 978-0-312-57048-4
  1. Time management.   I. Title.
  HD69.T54H644 2009
  650.1'1—dc22

                                                    2009024040

First Edition: November 2009

              1   3   5   7   9   10   8   6   4   2

To my first teachers,
who brought the power of slow closer to home,
Sophia and Jackson

Contents

Acknowledgments

The process of writing a book is a journey with many travelers. It is not a lone venture, but a meeting of the minds on many levels. The words "thank you" seem inadequate to fully express my gratitude to all the people who tirelessly gave to this project. At all hours of the day and night, they offered their vision, advice, and patience.

I owe many thanks to my literary agents, Scott Adlington and Jon Malysiak, for their focus, perseverance, and unbending belief in making a difference. I offer additional thanks to two terrific illustrators, Cathy Thorne and Vera Sansone, whose work captured my vision so beautifully. Cabaret artist Sonja Kling, through a chance meeting on a train to the Black Forest, contributed greatly to my early thinking about this book. I will forever treasure our blossoming friendship. Ute Becker deserves a huge thanks for her administrative and moral support. My dear friend, Donald Pillai, offered his infectious enthusiasm for the book, which sustained my own immeasurably. Without my sisters, Suzanne and Celina, and their generosity in answering my endless questions about how they view the world, this project would never have left its embryonic stage. From the Alps to the Appalachians, they tirelessly stood by my side. A special thanks goes to my mother, who listened through my tears to hear the possibility she has forever instilled in me. My gratitude goes to her and my stepfather for their ability to spread joy, light, and laughter in the darkest of moments. I am especially grateful to my father for his editing prowess and gentle prodding when turning awkward sentences into smooth ones and to my stepmother, who I know was looking over his shoulder some, if not all, of the time. My husband, who stayed awake with me as I mulled over ideas in the middle of the night, deserves a medal of honor for his limitless patience, love, and understanding. Above all, I thank my children, Sophia and Jackson, who provided boundless encouragement, counsel, and sticker rewards on good writing days.

To my editor, Daniela Rapp, whose humor, insights, and smarts kept me on track; to copyeditor Christina MacDonald for her spectacular eye for detail; and to the entire staff at St. Martin's Press, I say thank you for showing me dreams do come true.

Just as our relationship with time is personal, so is the path of completing a book project from idea to manuscript to bookshelf occupant. I thank the hundreds of people who contributed their individual stories through e-mail interviews, phone calls, and face-to-face chats. From New Zealand to South Africa to India to Indiana, you all made your mark on my thinking. Whether named in the book or not, each of you has added tremendous value to the end result. A gargantuan thanks goes to Peter Shankman, whose expert resource service, HARO, made it possible for me to find the world's best interviewees ever.

To you, dear reader, I extend my warmest gratitude. This one's for you.

Foreword

by Maggie Jackson, author of *Distracted: The Erosion of Attention and the Coming Dark Age*

Slow is hot.

In recent years, movements have sprouted to explore slow food, slow art, slow sex, and slow family living. It's a bit hard to fathom what exactly *slow* means in all these contexts. There's a bit of pro-green living here, anti-materialism, mindful awareness, community-building, all of which loosely add up to a slowing down in the tempo of life, or at least finding a speed other than high gear. The idea is hard to define, yet also hard to ignore at this moment in time, when so many of our complex, high-gear systems of life seem broken.

What's clear is that many of us have a deep desire to begin weaving a new tapestry of life. We're yearning to step away from the powerbar meals, hyperparenting, the distraction and blurred attention. We flip between people and tasks, keep one eye on the road, inhabit boundaryless alternate cyberrealities—and literally forget to *breathe*.

Whew.

What gets lost in this frenetic juggle? Moments of intricate social synchronicity. The unhurried conversations and interactions that are the lifeblood of human relations. A clear, vivid, sensual awareness of the earth's glories. Opportunities for the rich reflection that catalyzes all parts of our conscious and unconscious mind.

Slow is no quick-fix cure to life in the fast lane. But the "power of slow," to use Christine Louise Hohlbaum's gripping term, is an important starting point for recovering from these toxic ways of living.

As Hohlbaum explains in this intriguing book, de-accelerating is only one aspect of discovering the power of slow. Slowing down, in her view, is a process of recapturing time and revitalizing self. Step by step, Hohlbaum helps us to wean ourselves from an ineffective reliance on multitasking and a corrosive dependence on interruptive media. The power of slow helps us manage our expectations, our focus, our lives.

These are not easy adjustments. Refashioning our relationship to time challenges our creativity, willpower, heart, and soul. A good guide is enormously helpful on this journey— and that is what Hohlbaum gives us. With her lucid inspiration, we can begin journeying toward a new and better life—a life built on the power of slow.

New York, May 2009

Modern man thinks he loses something—time— when he does not do things quickly, yet he does not know what to do with the time he gains except to kill it.

—Erich Fromm

Introduction
Who's Got Time . . . and What Is It?

Have you ever tried to fight the wind? If you were a fisherman, you would know it is not possible to combat a force much larger than yourself. You have to go with it, not against it, to maintain your own equilibrium. You can certainly harness the wind's power with turbines and windmills; you can utilize its energy to propel yourself forward with sails and fiberglass. Despite all the things you can do with wind, it remains a juggernaut you cannot really control. We build our shields and protectors, but it is still there, an external power that remains a part of our lives. Sometimes wind can be so strong as to knock us off our feet, while other times it is barely a whisper on our cheeks.

Time, my friend, is no different.

Like the winds that kiss the ocean's surface, time is something human beings cannot live outside of. In fact, we enjoy a very close relationship with it, of which we might not even be aware. Time defines who we are. It is a reference point upon which everything else is based. Unfortunately, our relationship with time is a one-way street. We need time; it does not need us. Time's measurement is a construct we created to help us make sense of our world. The notions of past, present, and future are organizing principles to embed our lives in a linear fashion, even though time does not work that way. If you reach for a physics book, you will learn that Albert Einstein's theory of relativity states all things are happening at once, debunking our common perception of yesterday, today, and tomorrow. Physics claims time runs on a curve, not straight like an arrow as we commonly perceive it.

The notion of time dates back to our earliest ancestors who scratched on cave walls to depict future and past hunts. In order to be able to create those drawings, the cavemen had to understand that what happened yesterday is clearly distinct from what will happen tomorrow. In *Time, The Familiar Stranger*, J. T. Fraser, founder of the International Society for the Study of Time, notes how our handling of time grew with our own ability to measure it. Sundials, water clocks, burning candles, and clock towers are all human inventions designed to capture the hour. Despite our very best efforts to quantify it, time eludes us still.

While time itself is not a communicative device, the tools with which we measure it are. A clock "tells time," granting us temporal knowledge of where we are at any given moment. Time places us within a spatial context of our own understanding. We are either here or there. In addition to its relation to space, time positions us in relation to the events that happen within that space. Time provides a framework to help us comprehend the world around us. It helps us hold moments fast for future recollection. Time leads to remembrance.

Living in the ever-present moment, the way Alzheimer's patients often do, is not desirable, although as Eckhart Tolle tells us, there is power in the now as well.[1] Housed in history are the very artifacts of our existence. Timelessness is a state of limbo that leaves us without orientation or hope. Without hope there is no future, the very thing lacking in a timeless state. Human beings rely on time to frame their understanding of the world. It is a notion we cannot live without.

Our ability to tell time has become enormously sophisticated. We can measure "real time" down to a billionth of a second—the so-called nanosecond. While ancient Egyptians were grateful for sundials and water clocks, we have a mind-boggling array of time-capturing capabilities today. It is no longer simply wristwatches and train station clocks that tell us what time it is. Cell phones, digital alarms, and computers have joined in on the temporal fun. As pervasive as television monitors today, time devices are virtually *everywhere*.

We cannot extrapolate ourselves from temporal-spatial reality, as we are embedded in the here and now. Without going too deeply into existentialist argumentation, I claim in this book that our relationship with time determines all other relationships we have in our lives. It informs how we view the world, whether our glass is half full or half empty. It expresses our understanding of where we stand in relation to others. In short, time means everything, yet we mean nothing to it. If we were to divide our lives into the four stages of babyhood, youth, man- or womanhood, and old age as artists such as Thomas Cole have done, we would realize how closely linked our existence is to the passage of time. We are the only species with a conscious understanding of time and its infinite greatness. What is time, and why is it so important?

This introduction will attempt to answer these questions. It outlines a brief history of time as it relates to our contemporary understanding. It also tells you what to expect in the ensuing pages and acts as a guide for how you can make best use of this book.

What This Book Is ... and Is Not

Let's first talk about what this book is not. It is *not* a *time management* book. In fact, the term "time management" itself is contradictory. How can you manage something as uncontrollable as time? It exists whether we do or not. The only things you can manage or control are the activities in which you engage during the time you have available to you. It is inarguable that we all get twenty-four hours a day. And Americans live, on average, approximately 28,000 days. That gives us about 672,000 hours to make use of. While there are broad variations from one person's life span to the next, we all get to choose what to do with the time we have. Most of us do not know how long we have to live. This uncertainty makes our relationship with time extremely personal. We begin our lives with our own individualized bank account of time. It is up to us as to how we spend our temporal currency. This should not be confused with the "time is money" notion, which this book refutes. The claim is each of us has our own individual relationship with time and its passing. You can think of your life as a bank account with a highly individualized amount of time inside.

Looking at the world through the lens of our personal relationship with time, I have devised this book to be about *life management*. It offers ways for you to align your relationship with time so you can live life powerfully and to the best of your ability. I argue we must make friends with the only thing we possess—time itself. By developing a powerful relationship with time, we can also determine how we spend the time we do have. Take it from a recovering multitasking speed demon who always felt time was against her. I used to race through life at the speed of light, ticking off action items on my beloved lists and ever hungry for the next moment. It wasn't until I had children and was obliged to move more slowly that I realized how cool the power of slow truly is. The fact is we can all choose to view time as our friend if we want to.

You might be asking yourself what slow has to do with time other than its adverbial nature. In this book I treat "slow" as a noun. It is intangible, yet exudes a force so great as to transform your life forever. In fact, many people I interviewed as I wrote this book agreed slowing down is a good idea, but the thought of doing so left expressions of horror on their faces. They gave responses such as *"How on Earth can I fit it all in?" "You want me to do what? Go slow?" "Move over, Sally! I'm plowing through."* Once their knee-jerk reactions subsided, I could inevitably predict the pause in the conversation. They stopped shaking their fists, or moving their feet under the table, long enough to breathe. For a moment in time, they allowed themselves to evaluate their bulldozing mentality of time is a'wasting. "You mean I'll actually save time if I slow down?"

Exactly.

So let's be clear. Slow does not mean stop; it means to be mindful. The *power of slow* can be defined as the unmatchable force unleashed when you embrace your truest purpose in life. Mindfulness coupled with a positive relationship with time will make you unstoppable. This book is about harnessing your own power within and allowing it to unfurl. It offers you 101 ways to check in with your power without checking out of life. Time will help you do this if you let it.

You may find that some or all of the power of slow principles work for you. Others of you might find some obvious and wish to move on to the chapters that address your particular interest. Each chapter can be taken as a part of the whole or by itself. Brief summaries are provided at the end of each chapter to review what you have learned. You can skip around, reading chapter 2 at the end while diving right into chapter 9 at the beginning. I encourage you to take it slowly. Digest each morsel. Be kind to yourself. You are beginning a new journey to revive your relationship with time. As the saying goes, Rome wasn't built in a day, but remember: All roads eventually lead there.

What Is Slow?

Rome has been the showcase of many historical events including the rise and fall of emperors, gladiatorial engagement, and a bunch of wild animals flung about ancient stadiums and killed for the delight of the masses. It's a place, like many great world cities, where things have happened and continue to do so. Given Rome's greatness, it is no wonder that it was also the birthplace of the Slow Food Movement. In 1986, in protest against the McDonald's Corporation for bringing about what he considered the defacement of the Spanish Steps in Rome through its neighboring presence, Carlo Petrini formed Arcigola, the precursor of the Slow Food Movement that was later established in 1989. It was his response to the fast food restaurants that threatened to take over his beloved country's capital. Headquartered in Bra, Italy, Carlo Petrini's movement has spread to many corners of the earth. According to SlowFood. com, the movement currently boasts about eighty-five thousand members from 132 countries. The idea is to enjoy locally grown food that is cooked with care instead of ingesting what Geoffrey Godbey and John Robinson call "grease, salt, and sugar" thrown at you through a window.[2] With an eco-gastronomic focus, the Slow Food Movement later spilled over to other aspects of life including the Slow Travel, Slow Sex, Slow Work, and Slow Exercise Movements. The basic premise of all of them is that mindful living coupled with common sense impacts our environment in a positive fashion. Clearly a grassroots effort, the Slow Movement is supported by mainstream and peripheral groups alike.

Al Gore's efforts to save the environment from our collective carelessness have added fodder to the Slow Movement. Slow Travel focuses on using fewer resources to transport yourself from one place to the next. Taking a bike or going by foot offer solid alternatives to jumping in your car or SUV.

The Slow Sex Movement harkens back to the Tantric philosophy of hours-long lovemaking. In a world entrenched in speedy movements, Slow Sex brings about the friction without the quick grind.

While Slow Work has yet to catch on completely (or at least not many would really admit they were practicing it beyond their closest circle for fear of appearing less than productive), Slow Exercise has enjoyed a boom in recent years. Yogic practice, including Bikram or hot yoga, is not meant to go fast. The intention is to heal your body through pauses and poses, bringing mind, body, and spirit into alignment as you feel the earth's forces. Trust me. If you're with other sweating bodies in a room heated to 110 degrees Fahrenheit, you won't want to move quickly.

Slow is more than the opposite of speed. It is the wellspring of your being. The power you find in slow can be more overwhelming than the force you may feel in a German-made car whizzing down the autobahn. The attunement to your true purpose in life gives you the freedom to enjoy what you are meant to be in this world. Like any change, the process of discovery can require some adjustment. Anyone struggling to attain enlightenment will tell you it's not called *overnight*-enment. It takes time, the very thing that will help you live the powerful life you seek to attain. The results are most definitely worth it. What you will discover in the power of slow is your true self.

Founded in 1990 by Dr. Peter Heintel in Klagenfurt, Austria, and currently headed by Dr. Erwin Heller, the Society for the Deceleration of Time has ballooned into an international movement with a thousand members spanning from Central Europe to the Americas and Africa. During their annual symposium, the mostly German-speaking society gathers to exchange ideas about how to live more mindfully. Whenever she is asked to quickly wait, board member Angelika Drabert typically responds by saying, "May I wait slowly, too?" In her mind waiting is waiting whether you do it quickly or not. Angelika's personal view of time as a spiral led her to the society for its forward thinking about time itself. In each bend of the spiral we deal with the same issues, yet we reach a new level at each turn in the coil of our lives. She views boredom avoidance as a central contemporary issue around time. What would happen if we slowed down? Many think we might get bored. Stillness seems threatening somehow. Yet, as we will discover in this book, greatness is often born in the quietest of moments.

Slowing down long enough to actually think and become aware of your surroundings leads you to a deeper understanding of why you do the things you do. Building on that awareness, you can make choices that are much more powerful than those made in haste. Perhaps eating an entire plate of nachos in five minutes is not such a good idea after all. Maybe walking, instead of racing to the store in your car, would be the better choice. The power of slow is more than just work-life balance, although that is part of it. The power of slow encompasses your whole life's purpose by forming a positive relationship to the clock, to yourself, and to the world at large.

When someone speaks a mile a minute, we ask them to slow down. When someone drives too fast on the highway, a policeman says the same—typically with consequences in the form of a fine. The consequences of our collective urgency have left skid marks not only on the earth's surface but also on our own spirits. We cannot sustain this level of frenzy without reaching burnout, or worse, an incurable state of wanting. With never enough time, we are left unwhole.

Slow tells us to remember what is important. Sometimes important things require quick thinking and fast action, which, in themselves, are not inherently bad at all. You wouldn't want an ambulance to drive at a snail's pace or an emergency room doctor to contemplate his navel instead of jumping to your aid. There is a time and place for rapidity. However, this does not mean everything in our lives has to spin off its axis. Our 24/7 world offers us ample opportunity to engage at all times, but full-blown engagement *all the time* hinders living. As you will learn later, a record number of people today interrupt intimate relations to answer their cell phones. In fact, over-engagement without a true purpose is simply activity. Activity and productivity are *not* the same thing. To run up and down the stairs sixty-four times, carrying one crayon from your children's coloring box at a time, is not conducive to living powerfully. But many of us live our lives as if it is. Urgency, and its cousin, stress, are often based on fear—fear of the unknown, fear of failure, fear of the truth, fear of looking bad, or of getting hurt. We repeat the same activities over and over, expecting a different outcome. As Jennifer Louden, author of many comfort books, claims, you can only find comfort when you no longer collaborate with your fear. Working through it to a space of letting go will win you more time, joy, and abundance. It is not enough to take a day off if you are left feeling as empty as before. You have to stop supporting the very fear that keeps you up at night. If you find yourself unable to disengage from a time-lack mentality, reestablishing some ground rules is in order.

We can embrace the beauty of mindfulness while remaining task oriented and fulfilled. Like time itself, the power of slow is a mind-set. As Emmy Award–winning journalist Kare Anderson recently told me, she likes to slow down to speed up. In doing so, you will save more time than you can even imagine.

What Is Time?

Time is the organizing principle of our lives. The first thing that is determined after birth, besides the baby's gender, is the exact time the baby is born. Astrologists rely on that information to give accurate readings. Doctors and midwives note it down to embed the event as something "real." Time of death is noted as well, again holding fast to the proof of our existence. In between these two clock notations, we have a lot of decisions to make and experiences to enjoy. We have choices. To a great degree, we can determine how our time is spent.

Interestingly, we ponder what will happen to us after our deaths much more than what happened to us before we were born. It is this pending event of our own passing that contributes to our sense of urgency and linearity. As we grow older, we develop a subtle understanding of an ending we ourselves cannot foresee. You may call it impending death knocking on our door. Certainly, at some point we forget what it was like to live like a child in suspended timelessness. In the rush-rush of our days and nights, we wear our badge of adulthood expressed as the sudden lack of the very time we were born with.

According to the eighteenth-century German philosopher Immanuel Kant, time is both subjective and objective. J. T. Fraser follows Kantian thought when he describes the concept of personal history with its distinct beginning and ending of events. He calls our personal history nootemporality.* Fraser says: "It is meaningless to ask whether time is really *real*, as it were, whether there is anything in the world to which the idea corresponds. Human time (nootemporality) is intersubjective. That is, time is subjective for each person involved, but since it is an idea necessary for survival, time also becomes something objective."[3]

In our personal experience, time is something very real. Think of the many ways we speak of time. We can save it, beat it, lack it, divide it, crunch it, or count it. We can waste it, watch it, or enjoy it when it's "free." The reality is time *is* personal. We make it our own. Because we don't really know how much we have of it, we sense a tension as our awareness of its preciousness becomes more apparent. If this is true, why do we often treat time like an enemy or as if it were something to be beaten?

This book sets out to encourage your healthy relationship with time by raising your awareness of your commitments. Commitment is defined as the result of your underlying belief system that feeds your life's purpose. It's the framework from which you operate. Within that commitment you set your priorities, deciding what you will do with the time you have. Befriending time, not managing it, will set you free. After all, as we have pointed out, you can't control time. It exists with or

---

*Fraser makes the distinction between five different temporalities: atemporality (simultaneity), prototemporality (order), eotemporality (duration and distance), biotemporality (our sense of timing), and nootemporality (personal history with beginnings and endings). See Michon, "J. T. Fraser's 'Levels of Temporality' as Cognitive Representations."

without you. You can only embrace the time you have as you would your best friend.

We are moved by works such as Mitch Albom's *Tuesdays with Morrie*, which points to the wisdom of time as a friend. Morrie, a dying professor whose life-impacting visits with the author chronicle his newfound understanding of time on earth, reminds us all of the sacredness of life. Randy Pausch's *The Last Lecture*, which marks the life of another dying professor in both book and video format, inspires us to embrace the time allotted to us. During moments of crisis, time is never seen as the enemy, but as the innate treasure of humanity. In this book, I make the subtle claim that you do not need crisis to view life's marked beauty. It can be yours for the taking with a simple paradigm shift. Love time. Live powerfully within it. It is indeed all you have.

What Does "Relationship to Time" Really Mean?

It is hard to talk about time without referring to it. It is so deeply ingrained in our human consciousness that trying to explain something we live with and, to some degree, are a part of, is difficult at best. While we used to have a nature-based understanding of time through the seasons, we now look at time as something to work against. Athletes try to beat the clock; bored students watch it; factory workers punch it. Our modern lives have turned to divvying out units of time like Halloween candy, a little bit here, a little bit there and, in the end, we all seem to have a stomachache just trying to keep up. Inspired by Benjamin Franklin's philosophy of time as money, we have let our relationship with time become a love-hate one.

At some point, we jumped on the hamster wheel, dragging our children with us in their overscheduled routines that leave no room for the art of hanging out. Harried, rushed, and overwhelmed, a great majority of us run joylessly from one task to the next with an inner compulsion to get more done. The trouble is most of us do not even ask, "Exactly what are we rushing toward?"

This book calls for a paradigm shift in how we view time altogether. It is not something to be combated, but something to be embraced and enjoyed. We cannot talk about time without talking about work, as it is the very rise of the modern workplace that has made time the centerpiece of living today. This book will address many workplace issues as they relate to our temporal perception.

Much like an orchid needs certain conditions to thrive, we are at our best when we have "oxygen" in the form of a healthy relationship with time. It is a necessary component for a mindful, empowered life.

We can thank Descartes for his cerebral statement "I think, therefore I am." If I think I am under pressure, guess what? I am. Time pressure is an artifice we live with every day. While living on clock time is a relatively new notion, it serves as an organizational tool for our lives to run smoothly. With clock time it is easier for everyone to show up simultaneously to events. It allows for things to be scheduled, arranged, transported, or completed within an agreed segment of time. It leads to efficiency, productivity, and, presumably, a higher standard of living. That is, until you become enslaved by the very thing that once set you free.

Relying on the latest research, this book seeks to counteract our clock combat by offering solutions to time-robbing activities such as multitasking, addictive behaviors, procrastination, and always agreeing with others. It will also look at what we do with our free time and how to take mini-vacations for ourselves. Leaning heavily on principles of management, we will dig deeply into ways to manage expectations of ourselves and others. Delegation, distraction, and the last principle of choice are the final topics we will discuss.

Most of us believe being busy *every minute of the day* is a sign of success. The power of slow contradicts this thinking, declaring "busy" a four-letter word. It claims we must change our relationship with time in order to have enough of it. Each chapter, with the exception of the final one, will contain ten ways to shift our habits so we can "save time" while saving our sanity.

We needn't fight something we can't control. What we can do is embrace the opportunity to spend our time the best we can. Here's the great news: You have more power than you think.

This book will introduce you to the power of slow, an innate quality born in stillness, not frenzy. It will show you ways to integrate it into your everyday life. We were all born with a certain bank account of time. If we use it powerfully, we will live an enriched, amazing life. The power of slow can be your guide to get you there. May it serve you well and be the very wind beneath your wings.

The Power of Slow

Prologue
The BlackBerry Patch

The tortoise admired his shiny armored shell. It was turquoise with glittering bronze edges, the best model he could find that was worthy of the day. Stiffening his neck to appear more statuesque, he gathered his courage one last time.

"Today is the day," he told his reflection in the mirror. He buffed his claws with sandstone, then smacked his lips with a note of pride. Readying himself for the Final Race, he knew his time had come.

The gray dawn had given way to a bright mid-morning sun. The grassy knoll beyond the pond's edge loomed before him. Swallowing hard, the tortoise made his way to the nearby field where the forest animals had gathered. A nervous tickle swirled in his stomach. His confidence fell a notch.

Then he heard it: the thumping of sinewy feet behind him. Turning around slowly, the tortoise saw a shadow fall over his body.

"Ready to get whipped?" the hare inquired with a mocking tone. He shoved a carrot in his mouth, then wandered to the judges' booth.

"Hare E. Rabbit at your service. Let's get this race started!" The hare bounced back and forth in front of the judges with the confidence of someone accustomed to victory. He sauntered over to the starting line, then paused.

"Oh heck, Turtle. Why don't you just go first? Age before beauty, my friend. Age before beauty!" He cackled, revealing his carrot-stained teeth. With an inquisitive look, the tortoise lowered his head an inch. The judges nodded their approval. Without even a bang to signal the race's start, the tortoise headed down the racetrack. The hare leapt backward a few paces, then forward again.

"This is so easy. Lickety-split and I'm gonna win, but let the little fellow enjoy his moment in the sun. Meanwhile, I think I'll check my e-mail . . ."

The hare grabbed his BlackBerry, zooming from one application to the next. Before he knew it, an hour had elapsed. The tortoise was getting dangerously close to the halfway mark. He dropped his BlackBerry in his back pocket, then hopped forward to the river where the turtle had just crossed.

"Hey there!" the hare exclaimed a minute later, barely out of breath. The tortoise tucked his head inside his shell for a moment, then realized it was only his competitor, whom he had almost forgotten in his Zen-like plodding.

"Hello." The tortoise kept moving forward at the same pace. He had his eyes on the prize and nothing else. The hare laughed, jumping about as he had in front of the judges. Bored because the tortoise took no notice of him, the hare remembered he needed to make a few calls. He took out his BlackBerry again, punching in some numbers. He walked as he talked, leaving the race path entirely as he carried on his conversation. A family of robins glared at him from a tree branch. Thirty more minutes went by before he realized he was lost.

"Thank goodness this thing has a navigation system!" he cried, elated. Obtaining the coordinates, he soon saw his cousin rooting through the cabbage patch down the lane.

"Hey, Hoppy! Want to earn a few bucks?" He gave his cousin his race number, telling him to follow the trail to the end.

"I'll be there in a minute," he advised, picking up another call that had just come in. Hoppy jumped down the path, delighted to have earned some cash for nothing. After a few minutes, Hoppy got bored with running, so he stopped by the nearest tree stump and took out his GameBoy. "I have plenty of time to catch up. Tomorrow's another day!" Hoppy's eyes glazed over before he fell asleep.

Closing out his final call, Hare E. Rabbit toodled down the lane with his gadget tucked back in his pocket. He let out a yelp when he found his slumbering cousin near the stump.

"Gimme that race number!" the rabbit demanded. Hoppy awoke with a start.

"Uh, sorry, cuz. I-I-I . . ." Before Hoppy could blink, Hare grabbed the number off his chest. Just as the hare reached the finish line, he let out a yodel.

"I won! I won! I won!" The hare danced about with glee. Then he noticed there was only one bunny waiting for him at the finish line.

"Excuse me, sir." The little bunny blinked up at Hare.

"What do you want, kid? My autograph?" The rabbit stretched out his front paw to reach for a pen in his pocket.

"No, I already have the tortoise's. He's over at the pub celebrating."

The only audible sound was the pinging of Hare's e-mail notifications as he fell to the ground unconscious.

1

Time Is Money . . . and Other Lies: Ten Ways to Improve Your Relationship to Time

Cathy Thorne © www.everyday people cartoons.com

NO WONDER I'M ALWAYS LATE, EVERY CLOCK I OWN READS A DIFFERENT TIME.

Remember that time is money.

—Benjamin Franklin

In the mid-eighteenth century the world experienced a seismic shift in its temporal understanding as a result of three little words: "time is money." Benjamin Franklin's famous quote in "Advice to a Young Tradesman" is the guiding principle of the contemporary capitalist system. He claims that "He that can earn ten shillings a day, by his labour, and goes abroad, or sits idle for one half of that day, though he spends but sixpence during his diversion or idleness, ought not to reckon *that* the only expense; he has really spent, or rather thrown away five shillings besides."[1] Who would want to board a ship to Italy to visit the folks after reading that?

Accurate for the times, Ben's admonitions continue in the next paragraph when he goes on to say "credit is money." We all know that is not quite true anymore. Unlike time, credit can evaporate, as the world financial crisis has proven. Time has nothing to do with money, although your nine-to-five boss might have you believe it is true. Or perhaps you are paid by the hour, but you are still not paid for the time it takes you to move to and from your workplace or for the hours you sleep. Even if you receive an hourly wage while not commuting at all, it is not possible to translate all of your minutes into the pursuit of the almighty dollar because at some point you do have to get up and stretch.

Many people are paid a salary without overtime. No matter how long they work, their time is not equally traded for cash. What about volunteering? Standing in a soup kitchen for hours is work, yet you are not paid for the job you do. All the while, the rather misleading notion that time is money has contributed to our sense of haste. It informs our belief that if we only work a little harder, a little smarter, a little faster, we will enjoy wealth beyond our wildest imaginings. The truth is a lot of people value their time over the money they earn. If given a choice, 40 percent of those surveyed in a 1996 *Wall Street Journal* study found their lack of time far more concerning than their lack of money.[2]

Technological advances have contributed to our time-crunching belief that fast is more. Quick calls, dashed-off e-mails, and a whole new language of acronyms have altered how we work, play, and live. "BlackBerry thumb" is now a recognized condition by some in the medical community. The repetitive motion of excessive text messaging and typing on minute keypads can lead to joint injuries. Upholding the idea of faster is better, we often run through our days in a hurried blur of activity.

Benjamin Franklin's notion is embedded deeply in our consciousness. Living at the eve of the Industrial Revolution, he saw time and money in equal relationship to each other. You exchange your time for money, making time the new currency. Like the penny saved that was therefore earned, time became a precious resource to be saved as well. Punching the factory clock, we laborers bought into this system body and soul. But as writer and Web consultant Melea Seward says, "Old Ben wrote that way before the Internet." Today not all workers are obliged to engage in a one-to-one trade of their time for money. In some ways, the Internet has made time irrelevant. You can e-mail at any time of day or night; instant message halfway around the world; text message from the back of the classroom to the front; and phone over the Internet for free whenever you feel like it. Despite the time-suspending quality the Internet has brought to our lives, we still live within the paradigm of "time is money." Our contemporary tensions come from these two dueling principles: the time-is-money belief and the time-is-irrelevant reality fostered by our online connectivity. While we used to be dependent on store opening hours, it no longer matters if it is midnight when you want to make a purchase. You can still shop from your home computer. Never before has the push of a button caused commerce to happen at such speed.

Click the "buy now" button on your favorite online bookstore, and you put a whole series of people into motion. The warehouse staff locates the book; distribution packages it; the mail delivery service picks it up and places it in various vehicles of transportation. Another mail delivery service runs it to your desired address. The average delivery time is one to three days. What used to take weeks has now been compressed into mere hours. Speed has become the norm. Through it all, you don't even have to talk to a single person.

We have to reshape our belief that time is always money. The very idea is what Jack Canfield would call a part of our limiting belief system.[3] For many, money is considered to be the source of all evil. Consider this logic: Money does not lead to happiness; therefore, in the minds of many, it must lead to unhappiness. It is a part of our limiting belief system that suggests money is a bad thing. Truth be told, there is nothing inherently wrong with money, yet people often make it mean something negative. By association, time is placed in the same bad light. By the sheer nature of equating time with money, we place a cap on our earning power and put a negative spin on everything temporal. As a result, the clock becomes something we have to beat in hopes of tricking it to secure our own livelihood. For the most part, we have agreed upon the twenty-four hours a day, seven days a week system. But why do we need to believe our currency has anything to do with it? Is it possible to disengage our earnings from time itself? An entrepreneur might adamantly agree that you can. It is the reason many people go into business for themselves. By disassociating work from an employer's clock, they become more in charge of how they spend their time. That does not mean, however, that entrepreneurs spend less time working. Ask any business owner, and she will tell you she probably works more than before. The underlying freedom of entrepreneurialism lies in the freedom of choice, especially when it comes to *where* you spend your time.

Not everyone is imbued with the entrepreneurial spirit; however, we are capable of realizing the power the time-is-money doctrine has over us on a daily basis. It is a deeply rooted belief that, like Adam Smith's invisible hand, propels us forth every day.

Based on the time-is-money paradigm, Frederick Taylor conducted his famous scientific management experiments in 1899 to make factory workers as ergonomically efficient as possible. In an attempt to raise productivity levels, Taylor divided every movement each factory worker made down to the second, marrying work and the time it takes to complete a task for the first time in history. Soon the punch clock and punctuality became the highest virtues of early capitalist society. To be on the go was a new trend reserved for the elite. To own a watch was the sign of immeasurable success. And not much has changed over the years. It is no wonder, for instance, that George Clooney and Cindy Crawford are the faces that represent high-end wristwatches in glossy magazines. Who *wouldn't* want to be suave and successful like George and Cindy? Time and success are intertwined. The irony is the less you have of time, the more successful you are seen as being. Imagine a world in which the opposite were true.

Efficiency in itself is not a bad thing at all. In fact, this book makes a strong case for it. The driving force for efficiency, however, has nothing to do with money. It has to do more with a quality of life we all deserve in which feeling time-crunched is not a normal state of mind. *To save time is defined here as a principle to move our temporal relationship into a positive light.* We can manage a better relationship with time by soothing our own urgency and eliminating time-robbing activities that are out of alignment with our higher purpose. This chapter will attempt to offer time-saving principles that remove time from the money equation, thereby improving your relationship to it.

Principle #1: Personality Test

Instead of relying on the Myers-Briggs personality test or leaning toward a principle that thoroughly identifies the color of your parachute, I have devised a simple personality test to help you determine what type of relationship you have to time. It is not meant to be a scientific categorization, but rather a guideline as you examine your underlying beliefs about time. You may feel you never have enough of it or that you periodically feel time-crunched at certain times of year. In this principle we are going to identify your overall relationship to time by looking at three areas: punctuality, activity level, and your personal view of time. Notice how you feel as you mark your answers. Be as honest as you can when you fill them in.

1. When you are invited to a social gathering you:
   a. *Always* show up at least ten minutes *after* the appointed time
   b. *Sometimes* show up ten minutes *after* the appointed time
   c. *Always* show up at least ten minutes *before* the appointed time

  d. *Sometimes* show up ten minutes *before* the appointed time

  e. *Always* show up *at* the appointed time

2. When you attend meetings, conferences, or other work-related events you:

  a. *Always* show up at least ten minutes *after* the appointed time

  b. *Sometimes* show up ten minutes *after* the appointed time

  c. *Always* show up at least ten minutes *before* the appointed time

  d. *Sometimes* show up ten minutes *before* the appointed time

  e. *Always* show up *at* the appointed time

3. On the weekends, you spend the majority of your time relaxing.

  a. Always

  b. Never

  c. Sometimes

4. Do you have more to do in twenty-four hours than the time you have to do it?

  a. Yes

  b. No

5. You often say "I don't have time."

  a. Yes

  b. No

6. Generally, you would call your daily schedule:

  a. Jam-packed

   b. Balanced

   c. Easy-going

7. When you have to stand in line, you typically:

   a. Make friends with the people around you

   b. Look at your watch several times

   c. Leave the line and go somewhere else

8. When the clock says 10:36 A.M. and your appointment is at
   11:00 A.M., you

   a. Think you have fifteen minutes to get there

   b. Think you have thirty minutes to get there

9. You consider yourself a "multitasker."

   a. Always

   b. Sometimes

   c. Never

10. On your time off, you'd rather:

   a. Reduce your activity level

   b. Increase your activity level

   c. Stay the same

Add your points together using the answer key below to calculate your final score.

Answer Key:

   1. a-0; b-1; c-5; d-4; e-3.

   2. a-0; b-1; c-5; d-4; e-3.

   3. a-1; b-3; c-2.

4. a-2; b-1.

5. a-2; b-1.

6. a-3; b-2; c-1.

7. a-1; b-2; c-3.

8. a-3; b-1.

9. a-3; b-2; c-1.

10. a-1; b-2; c-3.

Results:

Easy-going: 10-17

Balanced: 18-25

Time-crunched: 26+

By taking this fun personality test, you will get a glimpse of how you view time based on the way you think about things and how you go about doing them. Note that the time of year may also impact how you view things, as your relationship with time is often cyclical. If you are a tax accountant, you may feel more time-crunched in April than in June. If you work in retail, your score will reflect whether you took it during the holiday season or not. In general, however, you will get a sense of how you view time overall. If you are persnickety about punctuality, you tend to view time as a commodity, something not to be wasted. If you are less concerned about your own arrival time to events, you tend to view time in a more relaxed fashion.

Couples therapist Elayne Savage works with people who often have different cultural backgrounds and temporal-spatial understandings. In her book *Breathing Room—Creating Space to Be a Couple*, she tells a story about a woman named Linda who is married to a man named Lloyd. Linda has a Mediterranean background in which people are valued much more than time, while Lloyd's heritage is British in which time means money. The main crux of Linda and Lloyd's arguments came from Linda's lack of punctuality. Linda was often late to engagements because her mother would call her on the phone at the last minute to chat about her problems. Whenever Linda attempted to cut her off because of her schedule, her mother would feel slighted. Clearly, Linda's mother has a more easy-going understanding of time than her daughter and son-in-law, who view lateness as rude and inconsiderate. Linda was caught in the middle of two time perceptions. She had to learn how to navigate the temporal waters so her mother understood her dilemma without offending others in her environment who highly value punctuality. She came to an understanding with her mom by giving her time limits when she would call at an inopportune moment.

After taking the above personality test, you are now able to define where you are on the temporal spectrum. You may be time-crunched some or all of the time, in which case the power of slow will be new to you. Or you have struck a good balance or an easy-going attitude, in which case the power of slow serves as a great reminder to continue down your path. The next principle will work with your perception to help reframe your relationship with time so you can enjoy it more.

Principle #2: Waiting Game

Waiting is not something we Westerners have learned to do very well. In our around-the-clock, instant-gratification world, we have grown accustomed to instantaneous responses through technological wizardry. In some cases, we are accustomed to getting answers in the middle of the night if we so choose thanks to twenty-four-hour customer-service lines. So when we are required to wait, it feels as unnatural as wearing winter boots in the summer.

In Billy Joel's famous song "Allentown" about the factory worker layoffs in Pennsylvania, he addresses the ennui of unemployment and the seemingly endless waiting required until life can begin again. "Out in Bethlehem they're killing time, filling out forms, standing in line." Waiting is seen as a time killer. As Billy so aptly states, life without purpose means time dies, too.

It might feel like time has ground to a halt when you are required to wait, but there are ways to be empowered as you do so.

I once sat next to a Serbian composer on a nine-hour transatlantic flight. The airplane was unusually warm, and despite a few pleasant exchanges, she eventually lost interest and began complaining about how long the flight was. "All this waiting!" she nearly shouted. Having grown up in a former Communist country, she told me she was accustomed to waiting, yet it had such a negative connotation that nine hours of sitting felt unbearable for her. In contrast, with a personal touchscreen and nowhere else to go, I felt as if I were in paradise. We had movies you could stop and start at any time and someone who served us food and drinks at reasonable intervals. I didn't see where the problem lay. In a rare moment of downtime without the kids, I actually saw the plane ride as an opportunity to enjoy some mindless entertainment and food I didn't have to cook. For the composer sitting beside me, it felt like an eternity.

Our time perceptions differ depending on the activity. In *The Secret Pulse of Time: Making Sense of Life's Scarcest Commodity*, Stefan Klein notes that our inner sense of time is very closely linked to the activity in which we are engaged. If we experience something as boring, time seems to drag on forever. If we think it is relaxing and joyous, time races by. The notorious saying "time flies when you are having fun" comes from our inner sense of time, which tends to be distorted by our brains. Various studies have indicated we are inclined to falsely calculate how much time has passed, depending on our own states of mind.[4]

Checkout lines are a marvelous place to observe how people handle the waiting game. Some people push their carts from one line to the next in hopes of joining the fastest checkout flow. Others stand patiently while staring at the racks of magazines. Wherever we are required to wait, it is inevitable that some will be more accepting than others. Where do you fall on the spectrum?

Einstein's theory of relativity claims that space and time are relative. In fact, he found that while the speed of light is constant in our universe, our understanding of time is relative to the speed at which we are moving. If we are required to wait without moving forward, we feel as if eternity is surrounding our heads like a bubble. When stuck in a traffic jam that inches forward for miles, we ultimately feel better than if we were standing still for fifteen minutes with only one mile to go. Our time perception is clearly linked to speed. The faster we go, the less time we feel we have. Conversely, the slower we go, the more time we feel we are wasting. To tap into the power of slow, you have to reach a balance between stop and go. It is about delving into the flow, which we will discuss in Principle #6.

But for Principle #2, challenge yourself to find joy in the simple waiting for things. Try to break it up into chunks. For instance, if you know you might have to wait an hour to see the eye doctor, tell yourself the first fifteen minutes you will read a magazine. The next ten you might write a letter or do a crossword puzzle. For at least five minutes, close your eyes and do nothing. Listen to the noises around you. Absorb the world from a new perspective, through your ears instead of your eyes. Be open to the possibility that you might just learn something from nothingness. In the stillness, you might even begin to hear your own inner voice, the whispering nonjudgmental one that resides in your heart space.

Principle #3: Time-Crunch Test

Nothingness and heart space? What does that have to do with time? In a word—everything. The power of slow relies heavily on your inner voice. According to energy healer Candace Talmadge our unconscious mind (the soul or spirit) and the subconscious mind (the heart or emotional body) do not interpret time in a linear fashion as the conscious mind does. "The emotional-spiritual parts of our being are our own unique time machines," she told me. "As long as our feelings remain unchanged, we continue to live in what our conscious minds regard as the 'past.' Only when we resolve our feelings does the self move into the now." The state of flow, as we will discuss in Principle #6, is the perfect state in which to heal our feelings to move body, mind, and spirit into alignment.

Our heart space often gets ignored by that part of our lives which is steeped in time starvation. Urgency has *nothing* to do with the time you have, but with the feeling that you don't have enough of it. By living solely in the past or the future, we miss the opportunity to live in the now.

Being time-crunched is an experience shared by many, no matter your station in life. In this exercise, you will monitor when you start to feel stressed and out of time. It is important to identify when you feel this way to see how much of it is within your control, and how much of it is not.

For the next week, note how you react when you feel your time is tight. What are the circumstances? Are you sleep-deprived? Stressed? Hungry? Overworked? Are there bright lights, loud noises, strange odors? Are you stuck in traffic? Late for work? Overscheduled?

At the end of the week, highlight the patterns you see in your time-crunched flare-ups. Point back to the first time you ever remember having this feeling. Perhaps it was when you were pressured in high school to get all your homework done on time. Or maybe it started earlier when your rigorous sports schedule in junior high crowded out time with friends. To heal these feelings, you have to identify the source of your angst. Write down everything you remember, including what you were wearing and the people involved. Once you have determined the origins of your time-crunch relationship, you can move to the present to change the things you can control right now.

If your time crunch centers around commuting, for instance, perhaps you can start carpooling or seek alternative methods of transportation. If you notice you start to feel drained by Thursday, devise principles of self-care to sustain your energy throughout the week. It might involve scheduling your more grueling

tasks earlier in the week or rearranging your schedule altogether. The point of this exercise is both to identify past-based
conversations about time and to start noticing the time-crunched
patterns in your present routine so you can counteract them.
Once you have identified your challenges, you can take action
steps to correct them.

Principle #4: Myth Buster—You Have More Control Than You Think

We have a lot more control than we give ourselves credit for.
Whether you are a business owner, worker, or stay-at-home
parent, you have more control over how you spend your time
than you think. While you cannot control time itself, you *can*
control the activities with which you fill the time that you do
have.

Freelance writer Alyice Edrich, owner of TheDabblingMum
.com, spends a few hours at the beginning of each calendar
year inserting important dates such as birthdays, anniversaries,
potential trips, and business-related deadlines, such as when
estimated taxes are due, in her planner. Instead of wasting
time tracking down information throughout the year, she has it
all at a glance. She saves hundreds of hours a year by investing
a few at the beginning. She may not be able to control what
unfolds throughout the year, but she has set herself up for
more "wins" by organizing herself from the start.

Throughout the rest of this book, we will talk a lot about
taking control of what you do with the time you have. While
many Americans spend their free time in front of the television, there are many more ways you can spend your time

powerfully and still feel as though you have enough of it.* In fact, researchers John P. Robinson and Geoffrey Godbey discovered the actual enjoyment of television consumption has gone down markedly in the past few decades, while the consumption itself has not. It is time to regain control of how we spend our days and nights.

Principle #5: Word Check

To paraphrase Shakespeare, thoughts frame our reality.[5] What we think is also what is true for us. We shape our world by the words we use, the actions we take, and the thoughts we think. Words have impact.

According to a time survey I conducted with a random sample over the course of seven months, 82.4 percent of the respondents claimed that, when asked how they were, they always or sometimes responded with the word "busy." The standard response used to be "I'm fine!" Fine has been replaced with a word implying out of time. Busy is the new fine.

How often do you use the word "busy"? Does it describe who you are, or just what you do?

In this word check exercise, review how often you say the following statements:

---

*David Croteau and William Hoynes state: "In contemporary society, the mass media serve as a powerful socializing agent. By the time an average American student graduates from high school, she or he will have spent more time in front of the television than in the classroom." Croteau and Hoynes, *Media/Society: Industries, Images, and Audiences*, 15.

According to the American Time Use Survey 2007, the average American adult spends 2.43 hours per day watching television.

"I don't have time."

"I'm out of time."

"No time today!"

"I'm soooo busy!"

"It's about time!"

"You're late!"

"Uh-oh, I'm late!"

"We're going to be late!"

How often do you use the word "time" and in what context? Do you ever find yourself saying, "Sure! I have time!" What comes up for you when you say you are just so darned busy? Share this exercise with others. Have a conversation with colleagues and friends about your busyness level. Does busy equal happy?

Principle #6: Finding the Flow

"Flow" is a gorgeous word. It not only rhymes with slow, but it also has enjoyed immense popularity in the past few decades thanks in great part to efforts made by psychologist Mihaly Csikszentmihalyi.[6] Flow is described as the state of consciousness in which you find joy in the simple execution of a task, often losing yourself completely in it. Art, sports, games, and other hobbies create a sense of flow in people who seek not material gain, but a higher sense of happiness in the act itself. It is not about a substance-induced state of nothingness, but an enlightened state of awareness of the now. While based on a state of doing versus a state of being, Csikszentmihalyi's flow depicts the weightlessness of life beyond the clock. The state of flow is desirable because you can enjoy a sense of time suspension. In flow, time is not money; in fact, time is made irrelevant by the experience itself.

As we will discuss in more detail in chapter 3, human beings love order. Flow harmonizes our abilities with our actions, thereby ordering our consciousness. Because so much of our lives is time-based, the liberation of human consciousness through flow injects us with immeasurable joy. We are no longer time-bound, but uplifted with the effortlessness of our task.

Susie Wyshak, creator of SuperViva.com, visits her friend's commercial fruit farm in the Central Valley of California with an intention to feel flow. She finds she can pick fruit for hours on end without noticing the passage of time. "Whether I'm picking peaches or cherries, or some other kind of fruit," she wrote, "being in nature amongst the shade of the trees, seeking the best fruit while making sure extra fruit doesn't fall, always puts me into the ultimate state of flow." There is something about the rhythm of the harvest that can put us in touch with our roots in the literal and figurative sense.

Flow can happen anywhere and under the most unusual circumstances. Steven Sashen decided to try Tibetan chanting after reading some simple instructions in a book he found. One evening around 10 P.M., he started slowly "swooping" between the vowel sounds: "*ah . . . eh . . . oh . . . uh . . . iiiii.*" The slower he moved between vowels, listening carefully for the barest hint of producing two notes at once, the more mesmerizing it became. When he finally decided to take a break, it was 4 A.M. The time had raced by so quickly because of the flow he had created. He even checked another clock to make sure six hours really had gone by.

Molly Roberts, MD, MS, and codirector of LightHearted Medicine,[7] engages in flow when she converses with her patients. "Flow creates a feeling of communion with each other and with the world around us that is very powerful," she said. It is so effective for healing that she even designed her entire mind/body/spirit medicine practice to allow for the time needed to literally "step into timelessness." As Dr. Roberts suggests, stepping out of time is an important aspect of healing your relationship to it.

To understand this principle, think about a moment in your past when you lost track of time. Describe the event and the circumstances. Perhaps you were playing music or your favorite sport. Maybe you got lost in a painting you wanted to complete or a story you wanted to write. How did it feel to be in the flow? How often do you "go with it"?

Suspending yourself from time altogether assists you in developing a positive relationship to it. You begin to realize that time, your faithful friend, is *with you* even when you are not *with it*.

Principle #7: Own Your Time

Aside from taking your watch off on the weekends or removing your clock from your central living space, you can enjoy time-suspension activities by taking time to go within. To decouple the notion that time is money, consider the value of hiking a mountain instead of sitting in the office staring at a blank screen, waiting for inspiration to strike. You not only get the necessary exercise to maintain a respectable level of fitness, you also allow your subconscious mind to work while you do something completely different.

Melea Seward recognized the value of owning her time when she was promoted from a traveling position to an office job with a major U.S. publisher. While she handled the initial transition from her urban Kansas City, Missouri, location to Manhattan well because her job was still traveler, just in a different territory, the framework of her day changed dramatically once she assumed a position as editor. Chained to her desk, no longer constantly on the road with its associated change of scenery, she was suddenly confronted with spatial-temporal sameness. The monotony of her office routine made her acutely aware of the passage of time. It negatively impacted her relationship to the clock, as she was no longer a participant-observer in her everyday life. She was as static as her office furniture, and she needed to regain control over her own life. In a leap of faith, she quit her job, which she had always thought would leave her fulfilled, without knowing what she would do next. After much searching, she found she prefers a more organic way of living in which work and play are integrated. As a result, she began to manage many different projects in various realms of interest. As a creative person with an impressive client list, Melea refuses to charge by the hour because her clients are in everything she does. When she takes time away from her projects, she allows her subconscious mind to work for her, even when she goes bowling with friends.

Your situation may not allow for you to go bowling instead of working on that spreadsheet, but you can integrate time-in moments to release yourself from the clutches of your schedule. It can be as simple as the no-watch rule on Sundays or refusing to check the clock when you are in your dance class. The trick lies in giving yourself some space outside the constraints of time so you can appreciate the actual activity itself. By association, you begin to reshape your awareness of time as a trusted companion instead of a party pooper that rings an alarm and ruins your experience. Time is there all along, but it works with you, not against you.

Principle #8: Gratitude

Besides owning your own time, taking inventory of that which you are grateful for can help immeasurably in raising your awareness about what you have. Gratitude lists are a great way to check in with yourself, to gain a new perspective, and to develop an empowered understanding of your place in the world.

Called "one of the most amazing people" he's ever known by Stephen Covey, professional speaker Tim Durkin told me how he experienced the power of slow while recovering from cancer. As he lay in his bed, he had an overwhelming feeling of gratitude wash over him as he realized how wonderful his bed felt to him. He started thinking about the person who sold him the bed, the warehousing staff, the bed's builder, the delivery personnel, and even the trees from which it was made. "And that was just the bed!" he exclaimed. "Don't get me started on the linens. . . ." His charming response to my question about how he tapped into the power of slow reveals a very simple, yet effective way to reestablish a positive relationship to time. With gratitude you begin to see the care other people put into the surroundings you now enjoy.

In this exercise, list all the things for which you are grateful. They can be as humble as the chair on which you are sitting or as considerable as your country's infrastructure. Whatever you choose, pick one or two items on your list so you can thank the person responsible. Maybe it's the UPS man who leaves the warmth of his truck to bring you your package or the neighbor who shovels your walk without saying a word. Be present to the gifts around you. As you are, you will notice how you start to improve your relationship with time as a friend in the here and now. You will see you have all the time you need for what's truly important.

Principle #9: Nurture Your Inner Muse

Creativity is not reserved for Grammy Award–winning songwriters and Hollywood filmmakers. Some of the most creative people I know are computer programmers who speak their own language and host a unique worldview. We all have the innate ability to be creative in our own right. Letting our creativity breathe opens up new avenues for us to establish a positive connection with time. As we go with the flow of our creative stream, we are buoyed by its sanctity.

Pablo Solomon, an artist based in Austin, Texas, steps into an enviable timelessness as he begins the creative process. "When I begin a work," he told me, "time loses its grip on me. My wife has to remind me to eat or to rest. There are days in which I work from the rise of the sun until late at night and never am aware of anything other than the sculpture or painting at hand."

Nurturing our inner muse requires a sacred space to allow it to unfold. Design a corner of your living quarters to house your creativity. It might be an alcove off the kitchen or a basement-floor room. Make an altar for your muse with whatever special things you can find to remind you to let your inner muse breathe.

While you may not be artistically inclined, you can feed your creative spirit by offering it inspiration on a regular basis. Hang out with like-minded people who value what you do. Join a book club or a discussion group. Delve into a topic of interest at your local library or set aside an evening to attend a lecture on something you'd like to learn more about. If you play a musical instrument, grant yourself permission to play whenever the mood strikes (and the neighbors are awake).

The point of this exercise is to give yourself over to the creative process. Suspend your critical mind by allowing whatever you create to be just the thing you were looking for. Do not judge the product of your creation, but embrace it as a part of the very process that will help you align your inner muse with time itself. Your inner muse shares the heart space with your inner sense of time. Aligning both of them is critical to establishing a positive relationship with time.

Principle #10: Abundant Thinking

Our patterns of thinking inform our experience. When we think we lack something, we do. Abundant thinking is the opposite of a lack mentality. As we have already mentioned, if you think you don't have time, you won't.

If we run our lives on time starvation, we wring out our adrenal glands for all they're worth. Feeding on a constant adrenaline rush, we teach our bodies that high alert is a normal state. If we slow down, even for a minute, we are confronted with our own speed addiction, which naturally leads to withdrawal. To avoid painful confrontation, we put ourselves back into time famine to ensure the necessary speed is maintained. Abundant thinking can remedy your need for speed as you realize there is nowhere you need to go. You have already arrived.

Abundance is defined as more than enough. If we lived in a state of ample supply, we would quickly lose the need for speed in all things. We would begin to see we are just fine where we are headed at a pace individually defined. In fact, we would find it acceptable right where we are. Human life is based on movement. Even if confined to a wheelchair, the inner workings of our bodies are in constant motion. Our heart beats. Our blood flows. We never stop moving forward even when it feels like we are at a standstill.

If you find yourself "stuck," that is a great place to be. It is the beginning of the end of your old ways of being. Awareness of where you are is the first step toward change. Bringing in abundant thinking can grease the wheel of transformation to bring you closer to the time you already have.

Final Word

This first chapter has introduced the possibility of improving your relationship with time by decoupling it from the time-is-money paradigm. We defined your time personality, explored the opportunity brought about by waiting, examined where your feeling of time crunch originates, addressed how much control you truly have, reviewed what time language you use, and placed you in the heightened state of flow. You learned that owning your time is better than giving it away, gratitude

helps you move to the present, creativity contributes to a positive temporal relationship, and abundant thinking sets you
free. We have established how you can nurture your relationship with time through the power-of-slow principle. Naturally,
you won't do all of these things at once, even if you are accustomed to trying. In the following chapter, we will look at how
to liberate yourself from the everything-at-once addiction by
busting the myth of multitasking.

2

The Myth of Multitasking:
Ten Ways to Stop Doing It

Trying to do too many things at once produces that jangled, error-prone condition that used to be called stress, but is now referred to as multitasking.

—George H. Northrup, PhD, president,
New York State Psychological Association

For many who are entrenched in the Protestant work ethic of diligence as virtue, multitasking has been hailed as the ultimate life skill. It is no accident that its popularity has coincided with the most unprecedented technological advancements in U.S. history. Now that we can talk on the phone while driving (in most states), or listen to select music while pounding the StairMaster, we've come to consider multitasking as an ordinary state of being. As a result, we've become so accustomed to dividing our attention between two or more places that many of us look for ways to combat the results of our frenzy: fuzzy-headed thinking and lack of focus.

In a *New York Times* article, neuroscientist and director of the Human Information Processing Laboratory at Vanderbilt University René Marois is quoted as saying ". . . [Our] core limitation is an inability to concentrate on two things at once."[1] If we are in agreement that it is not possible to do two things simultaneously, why do we feel so compelled to attempt the impossible?

If you've ever checked your cell phone voice mail while on hold on your landline, grab a number because you're not alone. This chapter looks at multitasking as a myth, the common multitasking mistakes we make, and how to correct them.

THE MYTH UNCOVERED

Multitasking can be defined as doing two or more tasks at once. The truth is it is nearly impossible to do two comparably difficult tasks simultaneously. While University of Michigan psychology professor Cindy Lustig and her team say multitasking is something we increasingly excel at doing from our late teens until our mid-thirties, the reality is multitasking itself does not help us do things faster.[2] A twenty-year-old brain functions more quickly than a sixty-year-old one because of age, not because of multitasking. Her findings show elderly people have developed so much internal chatter that they have more difficulty focusing on the task at hand.

According to some researchers, the attempt to multitask not only hinders our performance, but it also affects our ability to learn and recall certain events. According to a 2006 UCLA study headed by Russell Poldrack, UCLA associate professor of psychology, multitasking actually has adverse neurological effects.[3] The study cites research that underscores how distraction makes our learning less flexible. Declarative memory, that part of our memory that allows us to remember what we had for lunch a week ago, relies on the brain's sea horse–shaped hippocampus, which is responsible for processing, storing, and recalling data. When a task in the study was learned without distraction, the hippocampus was involved. When it was learned with distraction through a series of beeps, the respondent relied on the striatum, the brain system damaged in patients with Parkinson's disease. The damaged striatum is the reason why Parkinson's patients have trouble learning new skills while still being able to retrieve past information.

Another team of researchers found that we actually lose time by moving quickly from one task to the other due to our mind's need to rev up with each new task. Joshua Rubinstein, PhD, along with his associates David Meyer, PhD, and Jeffrey Evans at the University of Michigan, discovered how task switching can lead to up to 40 percent less productivity. It may be stating the obvious, but the more demanding the task, the less productive we are when switching activities. In a December 6, 2001, interview for CNN.com, Dr. Meyer is quoted as saying: "In effect, you've got writer's block briefly as you go from one task to another. You've got to (a) want to switch tasks, you've got to (b) make the switch, and then you've got to (c) get warmed back up on what you're doing."

Multitasking hacks at our positive relationship with time, putting us back into the hamster wheel of fear and lack. We try to trick its very nature of "marching on" by doing two or more things at once. The principles in this chapter are designed to work against our collective attention deficit by offering simple alternatives to our unhealthy habits.

Principle #1: Close Your Windows

Many of us come into contact with technology on a daily basis, whether at the workplace, in school, at the library, or in other public places. According to a Pew Internet & American Life Project survey from December 2008, 74 percent of all adults in the United States use the Internet. Much like television, computers have the amazing ability to pull us in. In fact, the organization found more people would rather live without television than live without Internet access.

A business colleague of mine once joked: "If my family wants to know where my time went today, I tell them to open my computer tower and look inside. They'll be sure to find the time monster eating away at all of it."

TAMING TOGGLING TYRANNY

When you work on your computer, only open those applications you require to get your work done. It's tempting to check out the latest YouTube video of your favorite singer/songwriter instead of dedicating your attention to your Excel spreadsheet. But toggling from one window application to the next is not only taxing on your computer's memory, it also costs you more energy and focus. If you're on deadline, close your other programs altogether, including e-mail, and concentrate on your work.

Gary Henry, founder of the Charlottesville, Virginia–based business consultancy GF Henry & Associates, remarked: "Each window and, more importantly, the application program (Excel, Word, Outlook, Internet Explorer, etc.) running in that window takes another byte (pun intended) out of system resources, mainly memory. If you have sufficient resources, performance will not be noticeably affected. However, sooner or later, with enough applications running, performance is impacted." He advises to close unnecessary browser tabs and windows. "Take care of your PC, and it will take care of you," he says.

Instead of reaching for the latest Web site quiz when you need a break, get up and move around. Socialize with colleagues or drink a cup of water. It has been scientifically proven that physical movement vastly improves concentration. According to Martin Seligman in *Authentic Happiness*, watching television, which YouTube emulates, actually puts you in a mild state of depression.

Remember: When a window closes, opportunity knocks at your door.

Principle #2: Thumbs on the Table

As globalization creates a patchwork of employees across the world, conference calls have enjoyed unprecedented popularity in the business world. Conference call etiquette is lagging behind the technological advancements, however. Many people multitask while on the phone, thinking no one can tell they're not listening. It's tempting to check your e-mail, shop for a new wardrobe, and generally tune out while surfing the Internet. If you've done this, chances are you've made a few mistakes along the line while not really paying attention to either task.

The simultaneous use of communication devices is extremely common. While the mute button can mask some of the clacking noises your keyboard makes as you formulate e-mail messages to colleagues and friends, writing e-mails while carrying on a conversation, even at a passive level, is devastating to your concentration. It can also make you appear less serious to the other call participants.

When chatting with a prospective client on the phone, Lisa DiTullio, of the project management consulting practice Lisa DiTullio & Associates, related how she could hear him loudly pounding his keyboard during the conversation. "The dilemma for me was this," related Lisa. "Do I address the fact he is not giving me his undivided attention, or do I politely ignore the fact he is writing while trying to converse? It became more evident when he lost his way during the call a few times, by pausing too long, or not fully answering my direct inquiries. I finally acknowledged he was a very busy man, and suggested perhaps we could follow up at another time when he was not so busy, and able to commit fully to the conversation."

Being busy doesn't pay when it costs you your professional relationships.

Jennifer Kalita, an accomplished D.C.–area entrepreneur, once revealed to me how her client, sitting across from her, pretended to listen to her sage counsel while sifting through his e-mails on his handheld device.

"Thumbs on the table, George," she wanted to shout.

E-mail is an incredibly distracting tool. It's best to turn off the e-mail notification window that shows up each time you receive a new message. A rule of thumb with technology: Just because you *can* doesn't mean you have to.

If you need your computer during the conference call, close your e-mail application unless it is absolutely necessary. Switch off your instant messaging functions to reduce your level of distraction. If all else fails, place your thumbs on the table, as George should have done, and count to ten.

Principle #3: Switch Off Your Cell Phone

According to *The Washington Post*, approximately 80 percent of the entire population in the United States has a cell phone.[4] Just think—240 million people chatting away their minutes, sometimes hours, every day.

Cellular networks rely on cell sites or specialized base stations to transmit signals to mobile devices across their network. While the term "cell phone" has gradually slipped into our vocabulary, there's yet another reason why it's called a cell phone— as if we're in a jail cell, we often feel incarcerated by it.

Dave Taylor, Colorado-based blogger at AskDaveTaylor.com, recognized how distracting his cell phone had become when his kids started saying, "Dad, can you stop playing with your phone and start playing with us?" It was an eye-opening moment when he saw how his iPhone addiction was impacting his kids. As a result, he has come up with tricks to limit its usage. By either leaving it in the car or at the office, he has learned to reduce his cellular fascination. Yet, the challenge he faces, like so many others, is that he no longer has a landline and thus feels unplugged without his cell phone within reach.

The Pew Internet & American Life Project relates how more and more people are valuing mobile over immobile phone lines. In 2002, 63 percent said it would be hard to give up their landline, compared to just 40 percent five years later. While 38 percent reported having difficulties giving up their cell phones in 2002, a full 51 percent claimed they could not live without them by 2007. The trend toward mobility and all its conveniences has taken hold. Mobility has its price, however.

Driving while talking on a cell phone is a prime example of potentially dangerous multitasking. According to Joshua Rubinstein, PhD, and his team of researchers, you need your inner voice, ears, and eyes to drive or talk on the phone. You cannot possibly use them effectively for both. Driver distraction is one of the reasons talking on a cell phone while driving is prohibited in many European countries where speed limits are much higher on average than in the United States. In 2002, the Harvard Center for Risk Analysis reported that 6 percent of all U.S. traffic accidents were caused by cell phone use while driving. The Insurance Information Institute stated that, boiled down into hard numbers, that translates to 2,600 fatalities and

330,000 injuries per year. While the Harvard study also said cell phone use while driving may have positive effects such as keeping the driver more alert through constant conversation, any type of distraction while driving can lead to a fatal end. In fact, according to a 2006 study by the National Highway Traffic Safety Administration, 78 percent of all crashes were related to driver inattention. Those drivers involved in complex second-ary tasks such as dialing a cell phone were found to be three times as likely to be involved in a collision than those who did not engage in such a task.[5]

The purpose of vacation is to relax, rejuvenate, and remem-ber what it is like *not* to work. Yet our cell phones have kept us in touch with the office 24/7, regardless of our whereabouts. There is even a Web site dedicated to wireless coverage com-plaints: www.Deadcellzones.com. The name itself connotes grief over the death of your connectivity. The Web site shows where you might have difficulty making or receiving calls. At the time of this writing, it appears parts of Montana and North-ern Texas have pockets of peace for those looking for non-cellular solace.

Principle # 4: Success Chart

Have you ever cleaned out your desk, only to find a key to your childhood diary, which you spent another thirty minutes looking for? You then discovered other treasures that led you in a circle that took you nowhere near accomplishing the task you set out to do. You may have enjoyed your trip down mem-ory lane, but the consequence is you're now farther behind in your day than you had planned.

A success chart can offset your lack of focus by helping you become aware of what you have accomplished throughout your day or week. While we often feel we're running on a treadmill going nowhere fast, we actually do get a lot more done than our minds allow us to acknowledge.

Jason Womack, president of a workplace performance training company, defines success as being okay with what you haven't done today. In other words, he places his focus on what he has accomplished and not what he has left for another day. If your ego demands you to show it what you've accomplished, feed it. A success chart can do just that.

Using an Excel spreadsheet, create two columns: to-do and done. Place your to-do list in the first column and the done list in the second. As you complete each item, move it to the done column. Alternatively, you can create a separate worksheet within the file to physically separate what's to be done from what has been done.

At the end of the day, review your list. You'll be amazed at how much you've managed. The goal of a success chart is not to cram more into your day, but to visualize your life as you live it. We are often compelled to do more than is humanly possible on any given day. Using your success chart will instill in you a sense of accomplishment and a handle on your own reality. It will also alleviate the time pressure we often feel under when we are overwhelmed.

With your success chart, you will become more aware of your completed tasks, thereby alleviating your sense of having to do everything at once. In fact, your success chart is the demise of urgency. Multitasking will meet its maker, literally.

Principle #5: Return of the Busy Signal

You're in the middle of a client call when another call beeps through. It's your mother. She's following up on the e-mail she sent you an hour ago, reminding you about this year's family reunion. The energy it takes to get back into your client call could have been used dialing the phone later to answer your mom's question. *Callus interruptus* plagues many of us. It's time to tune it out so we can tune in to what we're doing at the moment.

According to Telcordia Technologies, Inc., most wireless customers and about 90 percent of landline users today have call-waiting. Developed in 1972, call-waiting has become a prime suspect in our multitasking nightmare. (By 1987, Telcordia, then Bell Communications Research, further designed a switch-off feature with the rise of dial-up Internet access, because many people experienced interruptions to their data transmission. It was clear technology had advanced, but not quite far enough to help machines multitask.) Instead of focusing on the current conversation, the user was required to task switch whenever external forces told her to do so. Anyone who's been on hold while the caller gets the other line knows how frustrating it can be.

While call-waiting has its uses for emergency calls, many professionals I interviewed consider call-waiting rude.

"I never put business calls on hold," states communications expert Brenda Sullivan. A home office can be full of interruptions, but for her, call-waiting is not one of them. "Since I started working at home nine years ago, I have had it disconnected on our home line and only set to notify me if someone is calling long-distance on my business line (but I rarely answer). If I'm on the phone, callers are immediately sent to voice mail. I just decided that it was rude to answer call-waiting, and I didn't like it when I was put on hold, so I resolved to limit its usage." The only time she uses the feature is if one of her kids is calling or if she's expecting a long-distance phone call.

Even people in the business of people, such as public relations professional Henry Stimpson, question the multitasking function of call-waiting. "I used to use call-waiting for my PR business, but stopped because I didn't like being interrupted and interrupting clients or reporters to answer calls. Also, sometimes I'd forget to call the person back. I cancelled call-waiting and just use voice mail now." He still uses call-waiting for his home phone, though.

Designate one phone, such as your mobile, as your emergency line. Use the other phone, such as your landline, for non-call-waiting calls. As a further measure, deactivate your call-waiting when on business calls to avoid distraction and the temptation to multitask.

Principle #6: Eat, Drink, Be Merry

Mindful eating contributes greatly to the power of slow as you delight in what you are actually ingesting. You are what you eat, and if you are in a hurry, studies have shown you tend to grab what is convenient versus what is good for you. If you race through meals or multitask while you eat, you miss the opportunity to enjoy the very food that sustains you. Eating in front of the television, for instance, is a deceptive time-saver. You may think you are saving time by doing two things at

once, but in the end you will most likely overeat, thereby landing you at the gym for more time than you would have spent
if you had concentrated only on your food in the first place.

Americans, in particular, love to eat: that is, everywhere but
at the kitchen table, it seems. The United States Department of
Agriculture (USDA) reported an immense increase in commer-
cially prepared foods purchased away from home. While 75
percent still eat said food at home, much of it came from take-
away and fast-food restaurants. This trend has steadily risen in
the last few decades. In the late 1970s only 18 percent of caloric
intake came from food eaten out. By the late 1990s that number had almost doubled to 32 percent. People who enjoy meals
as a secondary activity (while driving or watching television)
tend to overeat.

Janet M. Neal, executive director and founder of the Professional Women's Center in Montclair, New Jersey, learned firsthand that eating while driving and chatting on the phone can
cause a major mishap. She stopped at a traffic light, looked
both ways, and drove through the red light with a motorcycle
policeman directly behind her. "As he pulled me over," she remarked, "I stopped all my other tasks to try to focus and pro-
fusely apologize. He asked me to step out of the car. I was
shocked and asked him why. He said he needed to bring me
in. I was about to burst out crying when he told me he was
kidding but would I *please* focus on driving?!"

A recent study by the Cornell Food and Brand Lab in the
Department of Applied Economics and Management revealed
the difference between American and French eating habits.
While the French, renowned for their fat-laced foods, rely on
internal cues of satiety, Americans tend to rely on external

cues such as when their plates are clean, their cups are empty, or the TV show they're watching is over. This strategy often leads to overeating and improper diet.

Another study conducted by Penn State University researchers Lori Francis and Leann Birch showed watching TV while eating impacted children's nutrition as well. Some overate while others ate too little. In either case, their internal cues were not observed.[6]

If you insist on eating in front of the TV, use portion control snackware such as the four-ounce Yum Yum dishes available at www.yumyumdish.com. Smaller portions will guarantee a lower caloric intake. Without question, the best method is to snap off the TV and return to the table. Take time for eating as the primary activity instead of making it a secondary one while doing something else. Your digestion, and your waistline, will thank you.

Principle #7: Mental Download

We all use our own personal tone to signal to people we're listening when we really aren't. In my tribe, we say "Uh-huuhhhh," extending the vowels to accentuate our desire to hear what the person is saying without really listening. It may be a mom thing, but I claim it's more a coping mechanism to deal with information excess than anything else.

Whatever your personal mantra of nonlistening, we all do it to some extent. It comes from our mental overload, when we are riddled with fear and a lack of certainty about an event's outcome. The result is often trying to do too many things at once.

The tyranny of our to-do list often leaves us breathless. In this exercise, you will need a pen and paper. Avoid your computer for now as it will only distract you. This exercise is not about speed, but about capturing what's irking you so you can move on.

Write down every single thing you're worried about. It can be phrases, words, even pictures. You'll uncover what may seem like silly things, such as taking out the trash on time or paying the electric bill, but life is in the details. And much of our life is spent worrying about them.

Similar to the success chart, this list of have-tos will help you download your mind and allow you concentrate on one task at a time. Scribble down everything you can think of that is preoccupying you. Once you have completed your list, walk around your chair three times clockwise, then three times counterclockwise. Doing so will unlock blocked energy. Alternatively, draw an infinity sign on a piece of paper, then take turns tracing it using one hand, then the other. Switch directions. Both of these exercises help connect the two brain halves for faster processing. You can now go about tackling each task according to priority.

Multilevel worrying can lead us to paralysis. Downloading our mental vision and adjusting our energy flow can sharpen our outward focus.

"Rather than completing several tasks at the same time," states certified personal coach Lauree Ostrofsky, "it's more likely that we're just *worrying* about all of those tasks at once. And not getting any of them done."

According to a 2006 survey of 1,600 adults commissioned by a consortium including iVillage and the American Psychologist Association, it was confirmed that women do indeed worry more than men. It appears women are not as easily able to hit the "off" button in their minds, so this exercise is particularly useful for those of us with multilevel worry syndrome.

Principle #8: China Plate

A sister syndrome to multilevel worrying is the "I can't say no" syndrome, which we will discuss at length in chapter 4. It comes from not having a mental picture of your priorities. The china plate principle will assist you in developing priorities and a deeper understanding of how many projects you can handle at one time.

The saying "I've got a full plate" is a socially acceptable way of saying you're already overcommitted. Taking this analogy a step further, consider your life to be a china plate. It can handle a great deal, but if you load it up too much, you start to see fissures in the porcelain.

Everyone has their own personal comfort level. Some people can handle up to ten projects at one time without losing sleep. Others can only handle three. Whatever your limit is, chances are you already know how much is too much without fully realizing you have control to say no.

Physiological symptoms such as insomnia, over- or undereating, nail biting, and an abnormal pulse will tell you if your stress level has reached unmanageable heights. A simple stress test can indicate what's right for you.

STRESS TEST

1. Does the idea of saying yes to the project leave you breathless?
2. Does the project make your heart *sing* or *sink?*

3. If you are uncomfortable taking it on, locate the reasons for your discomfort. Are you fearful of tackling something new? Do you feel overwhelmed by the scope of the project?

Answering these questions will give you clarity as to whether your china plate will bend or break.

Principle #9: Look 'Em in the Eye

We not only multitask with our lives, but we also do it with our listening, as noted in Principle #3. Shouting up three flights of stairs to your spouse is not a very powerful or effective way to communicate. Nor is it always best to fold laundry while your teen confesses her deepest fears. Body language such as direct eye contact has been proven to show people you are listening and offering your undivided attention. Staring at a computer screen while someone talks to you signals that you do not care to hear what the person is saying.

There are moments when not looking up from your computer screen is helpful because it signals to your busybody colleague that you'd rather not hear about the latest water-cooler gossip. Oftentimes, however, we prioritize our listening to exclude important communication, too. With children in particular it is essential to stop what you are doing, look them in the eye, and listen without interruption.

Linguist David Abercrombie considers English to be a stress-timed language. In his research, he matched the accentuated syllables of words to time-spoken intervals. He found that syllables in English are placed at equal intervals in time.[7] His concept of *isochrony*, equidistant linguistic events in time, can also be observed in classic turn-taking conversation, meaning one person speaks at a time. Small children tend to interrupt conversation, as they have to first learn the rules of turn-taking and listening. We all know active listening is an acquired skill. As their lives accelerate, many adults, however, would do well to relearn this crucial skill.

The few steps below serve as a reminder of how to avoid the multitasking trap while carrying on a conversation:

1. If someone asks for your attention, signal to the person whether now is a good time or not. One of my pet peeves is when people "talk at me" while I'm on the phone. Even if they whisper, they are still interrupting another conversation. Let the person know if now is a good time to speak. The same applies when you wish to speak with another person. Ask him or her if now is a good time to chat, then briefly explain what it's about. Let the other person decide whether to allow the conversation or not.

2. When you listen, look the person in the eye. Reduce the number of affirming sounds such as "uh-huh" or "yep" to signal you are listening. Maintaining eye contact is a stronger method of showing people that they have your undivided attention.

3. Observe turn-taking rules. Do not interrupt. If you do, apologize for breaking the person's train of thought to input your ideas.

4. Set expectations from the beginning. In a business setting, it is appropriate to say how much time you can dedicate to the conversation. If it starts to take longer than expected or desired, say "It sounds as if we need to look at this issue in more depth. When might you be available so we can chat again?"

5. Slow down. Rushing a conversation will most likely result in
   more conversation later. Structure your thoughts ahead of time
   so you know what you'd like to cover.

Above all, spontaneity can only happen if you are relaxed
enough to receive its rewards. Active listening and open communication are two means to honor your time and your relationships, allowing for unexpected beauty to unfold while you
shed your sense of urgency.

Principle #10: Gadget-Free Zones

In many religious traditions, the Sabbath is a day of rest. Or-
thodox Jews take it literally by forbidding any type of work
such as turning on the stove or flipping a light switch on their
Holy Day. For most people, however, that level of gadget-free
living is an unfathomable notion. Our plugged-in, booted-up,
interfaced lifestyle has us believing we are even more efficient
living this way, as if efficiency is the only end goal worth at-
taining. We live and die by being plugged in, however disconnected we are to the real world. Virtually speaking, we have
the world at our fingertips. Yet we are ignoring our most precious resource: our own time and the people around us.

A 2007 survey on public displays of digital insensitivity conducted by VitalSmarts.com shows that 91 percent of the more
than one thousand respondents have been more than irked by
inappropriate use of digital devices. In the study, Karen Schuh-
macher, a senior manager of corporate training in Cedar Rap-
ids, Iowa, noted the level of distraction her husband's handheld
device had on him.

"We were at dinner, and my husband was on his BlackBerry checking e-mail. When the waitress wanted our drink orders I couldn't get his attention . . . so I had to text him! That got his attention, and he got the 'message' to put it away."

Lynnette Harris, an editor at Utah State University, has found another way to unplug during mealtimes. "Having dinner together most weeknights and on Sunday is a priority at our house. My children are nine, fifteen, and seventeen so we've declared the dinner table a phone-free zone, no calls and *no text messaging*! We're together to eat and talk, 'live and in person' to the people in the room." She has caught her fifteen-year-old texting one-handedly under the table on several occasions. Once they established a phone-free rule during food intake, however, he relaxed considerably, realizing his friends don't disappear in the time it takes to eat.

Holly White Valliant, director of public relations at WS Publishing Group in San Diego, believes it's all about expectation management. She views her telephone as a tool that she can use, not the other way around. "People who know me know they have to leave a message. I like messages. I'm never taken off guard and can prepare information or whatever is necessary when I call back." And people have left messages, including several Oprah producers and Shirley Temple Black.

"The phone exists for my convenience," she said, "not me for its."

While you may not be inspired to send most callers to voice mail, having gadget-free zones is imperative to resisting a major multitasking environment. Common areas, such as the kitchen or living room, should be reserved for personal, one-on-one communication, not telecommunication that absorbs more time and energy than we often have.

Final Word

This chapter provided ten powerful ways to reduce multitasking in your life by lowering distraction levels and clearing a path for singular focus. Remember to close your windows, place your thumbs squarely on the table, turn off your cell, log your successes, flip off uninvited interruption during calls, turn off the tube during meals, download your worries onto paper, check in with your inner china plate, look people in the eye, and go gadget-free daily. If you implement these strategies, your multitasking nightmare will end. With its demise your new life is ready to unfurl. In the following chapter, we will get to the heart of our habits to see where all our time goes and learn how to recapture it with new strategies entrenched in the power of slow.

3

Creatures of Habit:
Ten Ways to Free Yourself of Addictive Behaviors

FEEL A LITTLE GOOD
NOW, FEEL A LOT
BAD LATER.

FEEL A LITTLE BAD
NOW, FEEL A LOT
GOOD LATER.

> Time is life itself, and life resides in the human heart.
> —Michael Ende, *Momo* (1973)

Human beings are order-loving creatures, even if your teenager's room tells you otherwise. A 2008 study by Northeastern University, which tracked over a hundred thousand unknowing European cell phone users, revealed that most people are creatures of habit. Those observed in the study took the same routes to work, to school, and to leisure activities, showing strong evidence of our desire for comfort zones and predict-ability.

Aside from the occasional lack of routine a vacation might bring, we all seek a certain structure in our day to keep us feeling safe and secure. In fact, most time management experts suggest creating a plan and sticking to it. Why? Because we all need to find meaningful form in our lives. Plans and charts signify ordered chaos and harnessed knowledge. They help channel our energy so we can make sense of our day.

Dr. Tina Tessina, a psychotherapist from Southern California, says we develop addictions when our pattern-seeking nature overrides the rest of our sensibilities.

"Repetition and familiarity are comfortable and soothing. When we're operating in our usual, automatic patterns, we are calmer, and life seems more manageable. However, this can become a problem when the patterns take over, and we can't seem to stop."

What starts out as a good idea, such as a glass of Chardonnay because you couldn't make it to your yoga class and you need to simulate the relaxed feeling you get afterward, can spiral into an uncontrollable habit that you can't live without. Most smokers know this to be true. Whether addictions are physical, such as smoking or alcohol abuse, or psychological, such as the overuse of technological gadgets, they cause us to engage in negative behavior patterns.

Video game playing, e-mail checking, or talking on the phone for hours are time-sucking activities that ultimately do not serve us. If you added up the hours you spend flipping channels or the days spent sitting in front of a monitor, you would find where all your time goes. The very things we do to soothe ourselves are the same activities that often turn into self-numbing, time-wasting tasks.

Internet addiction, in particular, has been the subject of an in-depth study by Dr. David N. Greenfield, a clinical psychologist from Connecticut who researches Internet behavior and its addictive qualities. "The very nature of the powerful attractiveness of the Net can foster overuse, abuse, and even addictive patterns of behavior," stated Dr. Greenfield. "Sex, e-mail, gambling, shopping, and gaming are some of the ways we 'get lost online,' and can contribute to problems in real-time living."

Similarly, Dr. Uma Gupta, an education advocate and president and CEO of Global Cube Consulting, studies digital addiction as it impacts learning. She defines a digital addiction as "an inherent, abnormal, and compulsive need and desire to use digital technologies, even when there is no apparent need to do so." Feelings of restlessness, incompletion, irritability, and anxiety when not doing a task are symptoms of an addiction. The sense of urgency that you will miss something terribly important adds to the addict's preoccupation. Anyone who has slept with a BlackBerry under his pillow can relate to that feeling.

Julie Azuma, president of Different Roads to Learning, insists on playing a particular video game with the television blaring in the background. She can't seem to make herself stop doing those two things simultaneously, and she has several friends who have the same issue. They are hooked on the feeling of toggling between watching TV and playing the game. She knows she should stop, but doesn't know how to go about it.

*   *   *

So what can we do to break the cycle? What changes can we make to liberate our schedules and recover the time lost through our self-destructive patterns?

We have to rewire our thinking. First, we must acknowledge our need for a certain set of patterns. It is in our nature to want to know what is coming down the pike. Second, we need to identify what our end goals are. We cannot possibly examine our existing behaviors without knowing what we are trying to accomplish. It is about raising our awareness to the kind of life we truly want. Third, we have to find alternatives to satiate our need for control while nurturing our inner spirit.

Forming new habits to reach our goals is not about self-denial, but about replacing what doesn't really work with something that does. In this chapter we will look at ways to alter our habits to feed our spirits and, ultimately, to reclaim our personal bank account of time.

Principle #1: The Habit Test

Obviously, not all habits are bad. You were probably taught that brushing your teeth after every meal and taking out the trash at regular intervals are good ideas. Most of your basic habits stem from your early years. But as we reach adulthood, we start to take on secondary habits that often arise as coping mechanisms when basic needs aren't being met, such as recognition, connection, or a sense of general purpose.

Brian Olson, vice president at Video Professor, Inc., gets up every weekday morning at 5:30 A.M. to read the paper and enjoy a morning cup of coffee. He's been doing it for years and feels incomplete if he doesn't get to fulfill his morning routine. The activity itself that Brian describes is not something he absolutely has to do every day of the week. On the weekends and during vacation time with his wife, he doesn't feel compelled at all to get up at that time, read the paper, or have coffee. It is habitual behavior that helps him start his day. It adds to his mental health and does not stand in the way of his getting what he wants. Brian has identified his habit as an activity that keeps him motivated during the workweek. His habit serves him well. It is neither harmful nor addictive. In fact, it helps him.

In this exercise, you will identify whether the habits you have are helpful, harmful, or neutral. To take the habit test, you will need five minutes of solitude. Go to a quiet space with a pad of paper or a recording device to complete this exercise.

In great detail, describe what you do during a typical day, and then what it would be like to change one of your routine tasks. Perhaps you normally drink two cups of coffee in the morning before you start your day. Consider what your day would be like if you changed the time of day before you had your first cup. Or perhaps you always check your e-mail before you have breakfast every morning. How would it feel to not check your e-mail until 10 A.M.? Try it out. If you feel neutral, it's something you could live without. If you feel scared or panicked while entertaining the thought of living without your "fix," you might be engaging in something that might not really serve you after all. It may even be an addiction that requires serious attention.

Ask yourself what the payoff is for engaging in your habit. How does it benefit you? If you can name more benefits than disadvantages, you are most likely profiting from the activity. If the opposite is true, consider this habit something you'll want to examine more closely.

Principle #2: Life's Purpose

How many of us begin the new calendar year with the promise of starting over? We'll lose that weight, rekindle friendships with former roommates, or clear the detritus from our lives. It lasts a few days or weeks, but we never seem to honor our commitment in the end. All the while we waste mounds of time chasing nonexistent rabbits down imaginary foxholes.

Why is this so common? Because most of us do not take a moment to identify what we truly want. If we were clear about our desires, we would have an easier time aligning our behavior with those goals.

The first step is to identify what your heart's desire is. To do so, write down all the things you've ever wanted to accomplish. The list can be as short or as long as you'd like. Do not censor anything. Be as crazy and as wild as your imagination will allow you to be. If you can't think of anything, recall your childhood dreams. Write those down.

Remind yourself that everything you write down is possible. Do not think about *how* you are going to do it. Think only about *what* you would like to do.

The power of childhood dreams was wonderfully illustrated by Randy Pausch, a computer science professor at Carnegie Mellon University who died of pancreatic cancer in 2008. In a memorable September 2007 talk entitled "The Last Lecture," he related how he went about achieving his childhood dreams throughout his lifetime. His unshakable spirit, drive, and focus accompanied him to the very end of his days. It is those same childhood dreams that serve as the basis for the part of us that believes anything is possible.

The goal of this exercise is to recapture that spirit with some deep thinking about what your life's purpose is. While this approach may feel a little uncomfortable, remember you are in an experimentation phase. You are exploring how you would feel if you shook things up a little bit to free up extra time and energy for those things to which you are truly committed. You are creating a road map to get you to your ultimate destination.

Once you have finished writing down everything you can think of, pick one of the items on your list. It can be as simple or as complex as you'd like. Take a new piece of paper and brainstorm about ways in which you can accomplish this task. In the same manner as before, write down everything that enters your mind, without censure. When you've finished, select one or two ways that seem slightly unfeasible to you. Then do them. The goal here is to bring you out of your comfort zone into a new space. If you are successful, you will amaze yourself. If you are not, you will have learned something. Either way you will have proven you can move beyond your own perceived limits. Return to your list and try a different action item until you find something in which you succeed. Continue to add to your list to encompass more and more experiences as you increase your comfort zone. Consider this list your life to-do list. Challenge yourself to see how far you can test your own limits. As you push the envelope, you will begin to see your life's purpose emerge.

Principle #3: Replacement Strategy

You won't ever arrive if you don't know where you are going. That's where your road map comes in. Building on what you learned in Principle #1, you can now start identifying the habits that don't serve you.

Utilizing a replacement strategy can help you kick an unwanted habit in a month. According to Dr. Maxwell Maltz's groundbreaking work in the 1960s, it takes people twenty-one days to make a life-altering change. His book, titled *Psycho-Cybernetics*—borrowing from a computer term that refers to our inner steering system and self-regarding attitudes—explores how we can use visualizations and affirmations to improve our self-image. As Dr. Maltz and many after him have discovered, you will need consistent focus to kick an old habit. It is best done by reprogramming your thinking.

First, take inventory of your daily habits. What do you do virtually every day? What is your routine? Do you check e-mail ten times a day or play a video game on your cell phone while commuting into the city? Do you listen to your MP3 player instead of listening to your spouse? Identify just one thing you might do differently, then try it out for thirty days. It may seem ridiculous in the beginning, but challenge yourself to take the thirty-day plunge.

If you check your e-mail every two minutes, for instance, start by setting a timer. Allow yourself to check only once every fifteen minutes at first. The goal will later be to check it at extended intervals each day. It is best to wean yourself off your addiction by replacing it with something else. If your office arrangement allows for it, do a few jumping jacks instead. Or drink a cup of water. You may find your new habit to be awkward or not as relaxing as your current one, but over time it will start to feel natural. If you continue over a series of weeks, you will have automated that part of your brain.

Replacing bad habits with healthier alternatives satisfies your need for structure without harming yourself in the process. You save time, feel better, and drastically improve your quality of life. "Having something different to focus on makes the psychological withdrawal easier," said Dr. Tessina.

Programming your mind to be attuned to healthy habits instead of unhealthy ones is a simple (although not always easy) adjustment. Your mind processes enormous amounts of information every day. To keep the information flow manageable, your mind filters out seemingly unrelated data while homing in on what is on the top of your mind. For instance, if you are focused on moving to Thailand, you will suddenly notice more Thai restaurants in your neighborhood, TV reports on the country, and perhaps even magically run into people who have been there recently. Similarly, identifying habits that cause you pain is an important part of salvaging the time available to us all. Once you notice what is stopping you, you can make a move to change it by replacing it with something more advantageous to you.

Amazingly, rearranging your patterns even slightly can open up enormous amounts of energy as you realize the innate power you possess to make a change for the better in your own life. It is not enough to consciously know that what you are doing is less than useful. You have to also act upon that knowledge to make the difference.

Principle #4: Identify Your Pain Point

We all have a pain threshold. Some can get their teeth drilled without novocaine. Others faint at the mere sound of the

machines at the dentist's office. Our *mental* pain point exists
in a visceral way. If you've ever woken up one day after grappling with an issue and said, "I can't take it anymore. Something's got to give," you've reached the pain point that leads
you to take immediate action.

Having lived in a house too small to accommodate the four
of us, I woke up one day and said, "Enough!" I reached for the
mouse, did some Web research, and quickly found a five-
bedroom house in our very neighborhood. It sounds easy, but
in reality it took us years of visualization, intention, and sav-
ings to reach the point of no return. After viewing the house, I
found a list I had written almost a decade before. It named all
the things I had ever wanted in a house. Every single thing I
had listed was in the home we later purchased.

David Bohl worked in the investment industry for years. At
one point, he was commuting from Chicago, where his family
lived, to New York and London, England, every week. During
a particularly rough flight, he awoke so disoriented that he had
to ask the flight attendant where he was going. He couldn't
remember whether it was Wednesday (London) or Sunday (New
York). That was his wake-up call to change his life from a
crazy hundred-hour workweek to a saner lifestyle. When they
finally sold all their houses and moved to southeast Wisconsin,
he realized he owned 120 pairs of underwear because of the
three households he had maintained. He vowed never to indulge his achievement addiction again.

David's pain point was the total disorientation he felt. He literally didn't know where he was going in his life. He just kept
running. It wasn't until he sat down to ask, "What am I running

after?" that this became clear. He now helps others "slow down fast" through his coaching business of the same name.[1]

Your pain point can serve you well. It is the mental mechanism that pushes you forward when you feel stuck in a rut with seemingly no way out.

If you reach the point of "something's got to give," you are well on your way to making a life-altering change.

Principle #5: Fight Feelings of Being Overwhelmed

One way to beat time-robbing activities is to avoid feeling overwhelmed. Consistent habits such as tossing junk mail before it hits your kitchen counter can combat clutter and an emotional deluge later on. Who isn't overwhelmed by today's demands, overscheduling, and constant barrage of information?

Besides controlling incoming information by doing things such as switching off your e-mail notification or your cell phone at certain parts of the day, you can also channel data by arranging for active, not passive, access. An RSS feed (really simple syndication) can complicate your life considerably. For those unfamiliar with RSS feeds, think of them as mailboxes you set up to obtain information. In this case, it is not mail you are receiving, but news. You open the floodgates of information the moment you click on the designated link to start receiving the feeds. Sometimes the feed software, also known as an RSS reader, is integrated into your computer, which is the case with Microsoft Outlook 2007. Whichever reader you select, you can start getting digital information in the form of brief stories, links, or blog posts fed into the landing spot of your choice. It is called syndication because, much like with a news syndicate, information is dispensed to various channels simultaneously. Depending on how many RSS feeds you sub-scribe to, you have the potential of a constant influx of e-mails flowing like the crawl you see at the bottom of your news screen. For many, the landing spot where the feeds collect is their e-mail in-box. Whoever named it "really simple" did not consider the impact it has on our daily work flow. The next thing we know we're reading all the incoming feeds instead of concentrating on what we need to accomplish, such as an-swering the urgent e-mail from our boss or actually feeding ourselves a good lunch.

The great news is you can banish the overwhelming influx of information by setting up a personal page on Yahoo! into which your top RSS feeds can run. Eliminate the feeds going into your e-mail in-box to avoid distraction. That way, when you read your feeds, it is the only activity you are doing in-stead of attempting to manage different scraps of unrelated data at once.

In Great Britain the nickname Worry-berry has recently made headway, referring to classic handheld devices that give you up-to-the-second e-mail notifications. According to a re-cent study conducted by the Consumer Analysis Group, one in three Brits feels they have less time now that personal digital assistants are a prevalent part of their lives.

Before you start calling anyone technophobic, ask yourself how much time you spend thumbing, scrolling, and pushing buttons in one day. Does all that activity really serve you? Most likely, you could reduce the amount of digital input and still do a terrific job. In a lot of cases, a high level of digital connectivity only serves to distract. Build in unplugged downtime in your schedule every day.

Tim Barker, a technology reporter for the *St. Louis Post-Dispatch*, appreciates electronic gadgets for their time-saving qualities, although he sees their limitations as well. As he related to me in a recent e-mail, we need to "take some time to enjoy the analog world. The other day, one of my sources replied to an e-mail, mentioning that she was at the beach in North Carolina, and how wonderful it was there. I thanked her for responding, but then suggested she put away her BlackBerry and actually enjoy the beach." Technology has its limits.

A wise person once said, "Just because you *can* doesn't mean you *have to*." Many of our choices make us crazy. Busting through the pattern requires us to unlearn certain behaviors and relearn others.

Principle #6: Breaking the Cycle Through Breath

Babies may not know much when they come into this world, but they certainly know how to breathe. Have you ever watched the belly of a newborn as she sleeps? It rises and falls in an equal rhythm. We are meant to breathe from the center of our bodies, not the shallow chest-centered breathing most of us do throughout the day. The lower we carry the breath, the more relaxed and centered we become, the better choices we make, and the more time we preserve for more joyful things.

"When you're feeling anxious or overwhelmed because of the time, your mind is going into overdrive," Dr. Adrianne Ahern, a peak performance psychologist from Nevada, related to me. "Instead of speeding up into a hectic frenzy, take a nice, deep, relaxing breath, and slow down a little. As you sense your breath going in and out through your nose and mouth, you are experiencing a moment of relief from your overactive thinking. You are breaking the cycle, and you are connecting with yourself—body, mind, and spirit. Take on just one of your to-dos."

The great news is you breathe all the time. The trick is to do it properly. Inhale and exhale ten times with an exaggerated slowness to bring down your pulse and release the tension that leads to our often frenetic state of mind. If your shoulders are stapled to your ears for most of the day, consciously bring them down and sit or stand with your back straight. As you breathe, fill your belly like a balloon. Allow the air to travel up to your chest. If done properly, your chest and lungs will expand outward, not upward.

While waiting in the doctor's exam room or sitting alone at your desk while your computer boots up in the morning, treat yourself to nostril breathing. Close one nostril with your index finger and breathe in. Release the air while holding the alternate nostril. Repeat several times.

Principle #7: Out of Sight, Out of Mind

Sometimes removing temptations altogether is the best practice to avoid addictive behaviors. If you recently stopped smoking, you'll know hanging out at the local bar with your smoker friends might not be the best way to handle your former addiction. The same principle applies to technological addictions. For example, if you watch too much television, removing your set from the central areas of your home will prevent you from being reminded that you even own one. Remove your television from your bedroom and living room. If you have the space, place it in a room specifically designated for watching TV. If you do not have the space, put it in your closet. The inconvenience of having to hook it up will probably be enough to prevent you from snapping it on while you have breakfast in the morning.

Any kind of addiction is hard to combat if you have the thing you want lying around the house. Hali Chambers's wheat addiction hampered her sense of well-being so much that she often felt puffy and achy without knowing why. A day without pasta, pizza, or donuts was unthinkable until she transitioned out of her city home to the country. The closest grocery store was thirty minutes away. This helped her to combat her addiction, because she stopped bringing those foods into her new home. It took about six weeks to fully change her diet, but during that time she dropped two pants sizes.

After one and a half years, she is convinced giving yourself a month to try a new habit really works. Once she knew how great she felt on the other side of her addiction, she was no longer tempted by wheat products at all. Sometimes keeping it out of your vicinity is the best way to stop your obsession and save you time by fretting less and living more.

Principle #8: Give Yourself a Break

Vacation is a great time to try out new things, including new behaviors. If you've struggled with a computer addiction, go to a destination without a wireless LAN or leave your laptop behind. If you really have to remain connected, make a deal with yourself that you will only pack one gadget. Alert your workplace that you will only be accepting emergency phone calls. Sometimes you will need others' help in the process, even if you think you don't.

RJ Cannon discovered how vacation can be used to break a bad habit when she surreptitiously started replacing her husband's nose spray with water during a holiday cruise. By the seventh day of the cruise, her husband, who had battled an addiction to nose spray for years, was using only water without knowing it. His wife had helped him disengage from his psychological addiction to something that was clearly not serving him. Although angered at first by her deception, RJ's husband grew to understand sometimes all you need is sun, fun, and water—and a committed wife willing to help you give yourself a break. He has been nose spray–free for over three years without a single relapse.

In this exercise consider how you might give yourself a break to alter your way of thinking and encourage more positive habits. Evaluate when you are most vulnerable to falling back into negative behavioral patterns. Devise a plan to help you when you feel the tug to indulge in an old habit. Sometimes the first step is simply sharing your struggle with others who can then offer you a new perspective.

Principle #9: Creating the Opening

The emotional value of spontaneity is not to be underestimated. If you have the habit of overpacking your schedule, you have no room left for the unknown. A recent *Wall Street*

Journal article suggests senior executives have more jam-packed calendars than ever before. In the face of globalization, they are often required to have face time with clients halfway around the world on a frequent basis. In fact, one of my clients went two and a half times around the world in six weeks, giving speeches to large groups. By the end of his marathon trip, he could barely stand. "At the time, it seemed like a good idea to agree to these events. Now I know differently," he told me. There is no opening in the life of a person who has every minute planned a year in advance.

Creating an opening means leaving room in your schedule for spontaneous events. Unplanned moments are often the most pleasant experiences as you allow them to unfold without attachment or prior consideration. You are simply living in the now, in an open space as life expands around you. Taking advantage of such moments lends a timeless quality to your day rather than the rigor of your nine-to-five grind.

Whenever my children say, "What should I do? I'm bored!" I challenge them to do nothing for five minutes. Even at ages eight and ten, they often can't sit still. They have grown to expect constant stimulation, planning, and structure. Allowing for unstructured moments, such as when a neighbor's child rings the doorbell to play, creates pockets of joy in an otherwise mundane world. It also makes room in your mind for creativity as you take a moment to rest, reflect, and withdraw from the unending stream of tasks that bleed one into the other.

Give yourself at least five minutes of spontaneous downtime every day. You may need it at varying times during the day on different days. Taking a quick nature walk, exploring a gift shop, or alternating the stairs you take from the subway to your work will help you create the necessary opening in your mind. It will remind you there are different ways of looking at things and lend you a new perspective. Taking a five-minute time-out will save you hours in the long run.

Principle #10: Switch It Up

The best way to change negative behaviors is to introduce new ways of doing things gradually. Habits are solidified in the brain when neural pathways are formed and begin to dictate your actions. According to brain research, your behavior is informed by the groups of neurons and connections located in your brain that tell you what to do. The only way to change your existing habits is to shift the neural connections. You can start in small ways by altering one part of your routine. It's not about willpower, but about persistence.

Switch up your routine on purpose. Instead of working out in the mornings, go in the evenings for a week. The point is not to change absolutely everything you do, but to try slightly altered behaviors to see what might work better. Instead of parking close to the store, park farther away so you get more exercise. Replace one soft drink with water or one cup of coffee with herbal tea. Much like creating the opening in Principle #9, you are freeing up your energy by trying on new behaviors. Remain nimble in your thinking by shaking up your routine enough to experiment with new avenues. Pretty soon, your healthier habits will feel normal, thereby replacing the older, less helpful ones you will gradually let go.

Final Word

This chapter examined how addictive behaviors stand in the way of our getting what we truly want, need, and deserve in life. It looked at how we can identify our bad habits, how to replace them with better alternatives, and where we can free up time to dedicate to the things we love to do. Through the habit test we identified which habits are positive and which are not. We learned to define our true life's purpose and how to replace bad habits with good ones. We challenged our belief system and self-destructive patterns, offering new perspectives of what is possible. We identified our pain point, selected ways to beat feelings of being overwhelmed, and learned how to break our habit cycle through effective breathing techniques. Removing temptation altogether is another way of breaking bad habits. A change of scene, such as a vacation, can assist in changing our ways. We also created an opening through which we can invite spontaneity and more relaxed fun. Sometimes altering your routine just a little is all it takes.

The next chapter will address how we can spend more time doing the things we enjoy by politely conveying to people that "no" is a complete sentence.

4

Power of Slow—Just Say No!: Ten Ways to Say No and Still Be Friends

WHEN I BEGAN SPEAKING HONESTLY,
THE FRIENDS I DIDN'T REALLY ENJOY
MAGICALLY DISAPPEARED.

Life holds one great but quite commonplace mystery. Though shared by each of us and known to all, it seldom rates a second thought. That mystery, which most of us take for granted and never think twice about, is time.

—Michael Ende, *Momo* (1973)

The spoken word is a powerful medium. Japanese researcher Masaru Emoto, author of *The Hidden Messages in Water*, demonstrated how the molecules in water are impacted by different spoken words. Because human beings are made up of roughly 70 percent water, what we say to one another affects our physiological state, too. The word "love" has a different impact on water molecules than "you fool." Using this awareness, we can find ways to say no with kindness and, in most cases, without using the word "no" at all.

The Dalai Lama is undoubtedly one of the most well-known spiritual leaders in modern times. His tireless stand for compassion and mutual understanding has inspired many of us to work toward the higher good. Always with a smile on his face, he is viewed as an ever-loving figure who says yes to humanity. But even a man of such influence obviously cannot accommodate every request. Ever wise, he too is faced with making tough choices. Apart from the obvious lessons of kindness and love I've learned from observing him, he single-handedly taught me one of the most important lessons of all: how to say no.

I once asked the Dalai Lama to participate in a project I was doing on world kindness. He seemed to be the perfect person for the role I was seeking to fill. I knew it was a bit of a stretch to ask him, but stretching the limits has always been my modus operandi. Just a few days after I sent the e-mail, I received the kindest response from his Dharmsala office. Admittedly, I had expected weeks to go by before I would get an answer, if at all. His Holiness thanked me for my kind offer. The office assistant explained his daily routine: four hours of daily meditation, a light lunch, then meetings in the afternoons. Understandably, with his increasing age, his time on earth is short, and he regrets having to decline. Now there's a man who has priorities and a great relationship with time!

It wasn't the rejection that impacted me. I almost expected my e-mail to get lost in the ether without the least bit of acknowledgment. What struck me most was the kindness with which he said no. He acknowledged my efforts, expressed his appreciation, and politely declined. A magic formula for saying no began to form in my own mind. It's about acknowledgment, boundaries, and clear intentions.

Underlying all of the principles below is the magic formula the Dalai Lama taught me by example. It is a three-step process involving acknowledgment, limits, and alternatives. First, acknowledge the person's request. It may be tempting to laugh out loud when people ask you to do things that might seem unreasonable or ridiculous, but in their mind they are serious. Acknowledge when a person approaches you with a request by thanking them. For instance, your neighbor has asked you to help organize a blood drive, which you've always done in the past. This time you have a conflict in your schedule or you have recognized it is not something you care to do anymore. Acknowledging your neighbor for his or her hard work is the first step in the process. You have a shared history, and it's important to let the person down easy.

In the next step you address your own limitations. You'd love to partake in this year's blood drive, but you have already committed to something else at that time. People may not take no for an answer or get upset that you should have known it's always the third Wednesday in July. Be firm. Stand your ground.

Lastly, offer alternatives. When people ask for your help, they may not realize someone else who is available could easily take your place. Offering alternatives is a solution-oriented way of taking care of the person's concern without drawing too much attention to your own lack of involvement.

*　*　*

We've all experienced rejection in some form or another. Perhaps it was a rejection letter after a job interview or a text message from a significant other calling it quits. Each one is a learning experience. Notice how you feel when you receive a message like that. Typically, we feel bad about not getting what we want. But sometimes we can also be inspired by the way in which people let us down easy. Keep the well-written rejection letters for later when you're struggling to say no. Emulate the style at first to feel more comfortable with the word.

The bottom line is this: When you say no to someone else, you are often saying yes to yourself.

Principle #1: Information Sabbatical— Let It Go to Voice Mail

Way back in the day when we didn't have answering machines or caller ID, we would lunge at the phone to be sure we got it before the caller, whom we could not identify, would lose hope and hang up. And if we didn't get it in time, our only option was to hope the person would call back. There were no keypad combinations to call them back. There were no keypads at all. Phoning was manual with either wind-up devices or, later, a rotary dial.

When did we become slaves to our phones? We still lunge at the phone in pre-digital dial fashion as if our lives depended on it. In fact, an international study conducted by BBDO World-Wide and Proximity Worldwide showed that 15 percent of the U.S. population interrupts sex to answer their cell phones. Germany and Spain landed at 22 percent of cell phone users doing this, while Italy came in at 7 percent.

Not answering the phone when it rings is another powerful way of saying no to someone else while you say yes to yourself, and possibly your loved one, too. Like setting office hours, you can also set phone hours when you are simply not available. Whether you choose to make them public or not is up to your individual style.

Randy Pausch, the late inspirational computer science professor at Carnegie Mellon Unviersity whose life was cut short after a brief battle with pancreatic cancer, had a brilliant way of dealing with his boss's request that he be available during his one-month honeymoon. He recorded a voice mail message that requested the person call only in an emergency since his boss demanded that he be available. He suggested they call his mother-in-law's house, as she had the number and could forward the call if she felt like interrupting her only daughter's honeymoon. He didn't receive a single call the entire month.

You may not have the flexibility to say no to that degree, but using voice mail to filter calls can reduce your call intake dramatically.

Principle #2: Make Use of Your Status

Ping-Pong used to be a sport. Now it's what your computer does when you receive an instant message, Skype call, or e-mail. In fact, we no longer write to people. We ping them.

At the time of this writing, Skype, the voice over internet protocol that recently expanded to the mobile market, had over 405 million registered users.[1] It is a cost-effective way of communicating with people, especially if you live abroad as I do. As convenient as it is, it can also be very disruptive if used improperly.

Instead of consistently allowing your work flow to be interrupted, make use of the status markers such programs provide. Skype has an array of status levels from "SkypeMe!" to "do not disturb." Instant messaging programs such as Yahoo! and MSN have similar features. Put your instant messaging devices on standby when you don't want to be disturbed. Alternatively, tell the person you'd love to chat at a more convenient time.

Kristie Tamsevicius is an entrepreneur who relies heavily on her Internet connections to conduct business. She finds the convenient access of instant messaging services to be a double-edged sword. On one side, it gives her virtual team members an immediate connection to her. On the other, some people take advantage of that service. She has learned to set her boundaries clearly, especially when dealing with a particularly challenging team member. She blocked his messages and tossed him off her list for a while. "Putting up boundaries helped me stop enabling his negative behavior. It gave him the space he needed to decide on a new direction. And in the end it was the best thing I ever did to help him. Saying no was helpful and the right thing to do—both for me and for him."

When used correctly, technology can screen unwanted messages and assist us in saying no without being harsh. We can use it to our advantage by utilizing its functions without remaining plugged in 24/7.

Principle #3: Saying No By Saying "Yes and..."

Sometimes you are faced with having to say yes to certain things, such as when your boss demands your attention for a certain project. In situations where you're met with conflicting deadlines, you can remind him of the other pending projects you have and ask for help to manage them by assigning additional team members to the job. In addition, you can agree to certain projects with a qualifier. "I can get that done if you don't need it until next Thursday," for instance. Alternatively, you can use an even more direct approach by saying "Here's when I can get this to you." Maintaining your confidence and communicating your ability to get the job done are important.

Your boss may not be aware of your conflicting deadlines. He may manage several people or an entire department. Having an overview can be difficult. Pointing out the overlapping demands and synchronizing with your boss's priorities can often lead to career advancement as you show an understanding of what's most important.

Oftentimes what's vital today can change tomorrow. Constantly shifting priorities can seem like a waste of time as you go from one project to the next without driving any of them to completion. If you are not in a position to decline a request, remember to qualify your response to manage the person's expectations of what you can get done in the time you have.

Gillian Steele, managing director at DePaul University's Career Center, recommends maintaining an ongoing dialogue with your boss. Key questions such as "What do you see as my priorities in the next six months to one year? What key deliverables would you like to see?" will avoid confusion and help you pursue company objectives in a clear manner. Gillian suggests confirming your agreement in writing.

"If you do this when your boss asks you to do something that has conflicting deadlines," she told me, "you can revisit your priorities by saying something like: 'This new project is going to affect the priorities we identified—which of the following projects do you see as priority? I want to make sure I concentrate my efforts on what is most important and deliver what you need on time.'"

Oftentimes, it's simply a matter of getting the clarification you need by asking a few questions.

Rich DiGirolamo used to work at a cosmetic company as a financial analyst. One evening around 8 P.M., his boss said she needed to have a report on her boss's desk the next morning. It would have required six hours of work to complete, meaning he would have had to work all night. He challenged the unreasonable request, which wasn't going to have any bearing on the direction of the project, by asking his boss: "When does this *really* have to be done?" After a pause, she said, "Sometime tomorrow." They agreed to table it until early the next morning when they could look at it with fresh eyes. In the end, they were more productive, completing something that would have taken all night within a more reasonable time frame.

"When you make everything such a priority," Rich related to me during a phone interview, "it makes it hard for staff members to give you the respect and credibility you deserve as a manager. Not *everything* can be critical."

Avoid reaching critical mass by keeping the lines open. Sometimes a no can be said with yes and a qualifying statement. We will talk more about how to effectively manage people's expectations in chapter 8.

Principle #4: Set Office Hours

When your colleague interrupts you for the umpteenth time, it's time to set boundaries. If you are on deadline for a certain project, let your colleagues know you will be available to speak only at a limited time each day. For instance, set your office hours from 8:30 to 9:15 A.M. Remind everyone you cannot be disturbed or expected to answer e-mail immediately for the remainder of the day. The more you honor your own time, the more others will, too.

If you work in a virtual office, strategize about your response time. If people are accustomed to receiving an immediate e-mail response from you, they will wonder what took you so long if you take a few hours to think about the answer to their questions. Check your e-mail at set intervals each day. Timothy Ferriss, author of *The 4-Hour Workweek*, suggests twice a day. Depending on how many time zones you deal with, it may be advisable to organize your batched e-mail responses around the most likely times your contacts would be checking e-mail themselves. E-mail begets e-mail. The more you respond, the more others will, too. To break the devil's circle, set your virtual office hours according to your own work rhythm. Answer your e-mails with thorough, yet concise responses. Loose ends tend to flap in the wind and land even more follow-up e-mails in your in-box.

Treat your in-box as you would your executive briefcase. With their rudimentary structure, Web-based e-mail programs are often difficult to organize, but there are other programs available. Microsoft Outlook is an application that allows you to organize your in-box according to recipient, subject line, folder, and so on. Whichever system you use, keep your in-box free of nonurgent items. File your e-mails as you would paper so that the number of e-mails in your in-box is never more than the length of your screen. You wouldn't schlep unnecessary papers around with you, so your in-box should be free of useless items, too.

Principle #5: Practice Makes Perfect

Saying no takes practice. Like any good actor you have to repeat your lines over and over again until they become second nature. This consciousness-raising exercise takes time, so be prepared to practice it several times over the next few weeks.

Set aside thirty minutes with a good friend. Explain to him or her about your intentions to say yes only to those things that really matter to you. In a relaxed environment have your friend casually ask you benign questions such as "Can you get my keys from the car?" "Would you hand me that magazine over there?" or whatever else comes to mind. Your response to each question should be "no." Ask your friend to respond in different ways, such as with indifference, anger, or laughter. Regardless of how your friend responds, remain consistent with your negative answer. Notice how it feels to block a person's request. Do you feel victorious? Guilty? Sad? Elated?

You can also practice simply saying the word "no" in the mirror or into a voice recorder. The object of this exercise is to challenge yourself to break your self-imposed limitations. Saying yes to everything is like putting yourself in a straitjacket.

Once you've gotten a handle on saying the word "no," practice terms that come across just as assertively without sounding harsh. We've all heard two-year-olds abuse the word "no" because of the reaction it elicits. Somewhere along the line we start associating the word "no" with really unpleasant experiences such as wanting that ice cream before breakfast and not getting it. Remember everyone was a two-year-old once so consider alternative ways to decline people's requests to avoid negative reactions. Below is a list of positive statements you may wish to tailor to your own situation.

Practice Statements for Saying No with Kindness

"Thank you so much for asking. I'm unavailable at that time."

"It sounds like a terrific opportunity that I'm going to miss."

"What a neat idea! To honor the integrity of my commitments, I have to decline right now. I appreciate your thinking of me!"

"I am so honored you've asked. Unfortunately, I have an overlapping commitment that day. Thank you anyway!"

Principle #6: Stick with the KISS (Keep It Simple, Silly)

Once you have practiced saying no in a safe environment, you can begin testing the waters with real people in your life. You need not make excuses when declining people's requests. You also needn't apologize for safeguarding your time. Remember, you've worked hard to establish a positive relationship with time. Now is not the time to blow it by overcommitting yourself.

Guilt often coincides with our saying no to people. Our knee-jerk reaction is to acquiesce because it's simpler that way. When you say yes, you don't have to explain, the person responds favorably to your agreeing nature, and for a single moment, you feel good—until you realize you actually didn't want to agree in the first place. This principle of keeping your response simple can help those who suffer from the people-pleasing syndrome. The KISS approach requires no explanation at all.

If someone approaches you with a request, you can respond by saying, "Thank you for thinking of me, but I'm going to have to decline." If the person presses you, you can respond by suggesting an alternative: "Mary loves music. Perhaps she can help you organize the charity orchestra event!" Oftentimes we get blindsided by people's out-of-the-blue requests. Keep the term "We have a prior commitment" on tap for those times you can't think of anything else to say.

Sometimes you need a team of people to support you while you learn the ropes. Former Delray Beach, Florida, mayor Jeff Perlman had a habit of agreeing to even the simplest tasks, such as attending the opening of a new telephone booth. It was only when he realized he couldn't fulfill his objectives for the community that he had to put a stop to his insane work schedule. He wrote down his core values for the city and for himself. If he received a request that did not align with those values, he denied the request. Later on he employed his staff and his wife to be his gatekeepers. He no longer accommodated people's requests, on the phone or in person. His standard line was that he had to check his calendar first.

Creating a little distance between yourself and others can mean the difference between no and yes. Using simple yet effective language can help you maintain the balance in your relationships while giving you the backbone to preserve yourself in the process.

Mellanie True Hills, author of *A Woman's Guide to Saving Her Own Life*, almost died from saying yes too much. During the high-flying '90s, she was living a 24/7 existence in the high-tech industry as an Internet visionary. After she landed in the hospital for emergency heart surgery, she realized she had to reevaluate how she was living her life. She could no longer keep up with the impossible demands and her yea-saying was literally killing her. A weight loss program and a change of jobs brought sanity back into her life. Saying no became an integral part of her new system. While she was serving as a volunteer for four nonprofits, a fifth organization approached her to do some work for them. Honoring her new life commitment, she politely declined.

"You can let them know that you are not saying no to them personally, but to a task that you just can't do due to other commitments," she wrote. "For your health, you just can't accept anything more at this time. Let them know you're honored or humbled to be asked, and would love to do so, but just can't right now. Maybe later. And you want to still be friends." She has learned the art of negotiation and setting boundaries without sacrificing excellence or her health.

As vice president of marketing for a Kansas-based development company, Ann Keefer follows a "no vampire rule" that has worked well for her for over a decade. If something is emotionally, financially, or spiritually draining, she says no quickly and without explanation. To pass the test, she has a two-question approach.

1. Will it serve me or others?
2. Can I spend adequate time to complete the request?

If the answer is yes to both, she accepts the challenge. Otherwise, she moves on.

Principle #7: Be Your Word

The surest way to dilute your credibility is to say one thing and then do another. Not doing what you say you will do leads people to disbelieve you in the future. If you say you are unplugging during your week's vacation but then answer voice mails and e-mails, you are not being your word. You teach people that your personal time is not really your own. They can barge in any time they feel like it because you yourself blur the lines. Being your word is simply keeping what you *say* and what you *do* in alignment.

In *The Four Agreements*, author Don Miguel Ruiz lists four life philosophies rooted in the Toltec tradition that, if observed, can lead to a more empowered life. "Be your word" is the first agreement. In fact, besides the time you are born with, all you have is your word.

Much like in parenting, a large part of saying no is consistency. If people can count on you to do what you say you will do, saying no will come easier, as they have come to rely on your word as truth. It can be expressed by using an autoresponder to state the times you are online to manage your e-mail traffic. If you teach people how to treat you by being consistent and your word, it will eliminate explanation almost entirely.

Executive coach and speaker Victoria Trabosh was twenty-three when she fell in love with a man eighteen years her senior. A single dad raising four teenagers, her then-boyfriend was rejected by all her friends and family. Without listening to all the nos around her, Victoria married him anyway. She applied the wisdom her mother had passed on to her years before. "If you can say yes with all your heart, then go for it." Her mother taught her the meaning of commitment and the power of her word. Almost three decades later they are still happily married, grateful each day that they said no to others while saying yes to themselves.

Principle #8: Declining with a Compliment

As the Dalai Lama so aptly showed me, declining an invitation needn't be a painful experience. Showing interest in the person's social event, for instance, eases the disappointment by laying the focus on the host or hostess. Vera Stanfield, the wife of a retired Navy chaplain in San Diego, California, suggests concentrating on the event and drawing attention away from the reason you cannot attend. Instead of an apology, she offers a compliment: "I say, 'Oh, I know it will be a wonderful party, and we are disappointed to miss out on the fun, but we have a conflict on that date. You always make your guests feel so welcome and entertain beautifully. What will you be serving?

Who else will be able to join in the fun? I'm sure it will be lovely; we will be anxious to hear all about it.'" Who could be mad after being so flattered?

Another added bonus to saying no with kindness is how it impacts those around you. You will inspire others to be honest about their own priorities, including your own family. According to Geralin Thomas, a certified professional organizer and owner of Metropolitan Organizing, your children will see your prioritizing as an example to follow in their own lives. "When your children hear you prioritizing family times, they learn to respect the idea of scheduling tasks; in addition, they learn to set their own boundaries. The biggest bonus? They understand that 'I love you' means slowing down enough to spend time together as a family."

Note how other people say no with a smile. Emulate their response until it feels natural for you, too.

Principle#9: Saying No to Yourself Is a Yes to Your Commitment

We have already established that saying no is a delicate thing. It's hard enough to say no to others, but having to say it to ourselves can be even worse: Just one more glass of wine, television show, video game—fill in the blank. We justify ourselves by saying we need it. In reality, what we need is often very different.

David Bohl of Slowdownfast.com embraced a healthier lifestyle after realizing he had an issue with alcohol. He learned to say no in social situations by telling his friends he had had enough drinks for a lifetime. He was also an achievement addict who frequently worked long hours while neglecting his family. He now takes on fewer projects and sees it as saying yes to his family life.

Neil Gussman, a bike racer with a reputation for always showing up for training, sustained a serious back injury during a bike race that landed him in a neck and chest brace for weeks. Due to his lack of mobility, he started to gain weight, which he later lost with the help of a weight loss support group. He found it best to look at his weight loss challenge as saying yes to his commitment to physical fitness and health instead of no to the salty bag of chips at night. To carry him through, he looked to other people who faced the same struggle. It helped him maintain a level of resolve he would not have otherwise had.

Look outside yourself to find commitments you can say yes to instead of focusing on the negative. As we will see in chapter 9, focusing on what you want versus what you don't want will help you achieve your objectives.

As we discussed in chapter 3, bad habits can lead to time-sucking activities or, as relationship expert Catherine Behan says, "energy bandits" that steal your energy and, most regularly, your money, too. As a former shopaholic, Catherine has learned to curb her impulsive online shopping ways by creating a ranking system for the things she wants to purchase. She uses a scale from one to ten and never considers buying anything under a six. She also has replaced her shopping buzz with mood energizers such as music that reminds her of the good times. "Sifting through my emotional reactions to hearing myself say no, I have uncovered a lot of energy bandits. Energy bandits kidnapped me and held me trapped in a single-minded thought pattern that sounded something like this: 'The only way to have fun is to buy something.' Out of touch with my intuition, I found myself buying things that weren't quite right, never got used, and eventually were given away." She now only goes for the nines and tens. It is a system that has worked well. It's unleashed a lot of energy, saved her money and, in the end, time itself.

Principle #10: Listen First

Active listening does not mean you nod your head and mumble "yes" every few seconds. In fact, eliminating the learned trappings of "listening" removes the distracting quality of your body language. If you are face-to-face with someone, stand or sit straight *without* your arms crossed. This signals to the speaker that you are open to what he or she has to say. As we mentioned in chapter 2, looking away from your computer monitor and at the person talking shows you care about the person. It also helps you keep your focus on what the person is truly asking. Most often when people make a request, it stems from their belief in your ability. You may be thinking your co-worker just wants to slough off undesirable projects onto you. Deep down they are most likely thinking you could do it better anyway.

Saying no involves some level of alienation. In the act of declining, we are separating ourselves from the person's wishes, so it requires a certain level of grace, especially in the workplace. Senior innovation manager Beril Altiner works at a convenience tableware company near Chicago. Her major concern at work has been aligning her desire to be a team player with her need to say no in instances where a project may be going down a path that could compromise the time line. She practices active listening, occasionally asking questions to probe deeper into the real issue at hand. "At the end of the discussion I say something like 'I see where you're coming from and that's a valid point, but here is what concerns me about what you're suggesting.' I then go on to explain it." This usually results in her team coming up with a more effective solution that avoids unnecessary busywork for all involved and meets the company's needs.

Listening also gives you time to consider other options. By not reacting immediately, you can let the person's words sink in. Sometimes the silence between words holds more weight than the hot air you might fill it with. This strategy is particularly useful with people who consistently make outrageous demands. It gives them time to hear themselves, something they might not do often. Offer them the opportunity to listen to their own requests by saying nothing.

Final Word

This chapter gave you an overview of how to approach sticky situations with kindness. Declining invitations, demands, and unreasonable requests can save you a bucket of time as you focus on what matters to you. While there are more than ten ways to say no, the ways we explored here include taking an information sabbatical by letting your calls go to voice mail, managing your status when using instant messaging tools, clarifying priorities in the workplace by using qualifying statements, setting office hours to signal availability, practicing the word "no" with friends and colleagues, keeping it simple without guilt, honoring your word, declining with a compliment, remembering your commitments, and listening above all else.

You're now starting to tap into the power of slow. You are beginning to realize you don't have to do it all to have it all. In the next chapter we will look at how going slow doesn't mean you stop. Leave your ticket to procrastination station behind. There's a more powerful destination down the tracks.

5

Procrastination Station: Ten Ways to Move Forward When You Just Don't Want To

Procrastination is the thief of time.

—Edward Young, English poet (1742)

What would happen if a train, scheduled to leave in the nick of time for you to make it to your sister's wedding on the Jersey Shore, decided it just wasn't going to leave that day. The sun was shining, its tracks had just been cleaned, and frankly, it was tired of hauling ungrateful people who filled its trash cans with fouling banana peels up and down the East Coast. It knew it should get going, get you there on time, and do its duty. But its own sense of feeling overwhelmed and its fear of not getting it right kept it from moving even an inch. You forgo your ticket money. You don't get there on time. Welcome to procrastination station.

In the real world, procrastination costs people more than just money, time, and productivity. It costs us health and happiness, too. Guilt, regret, and a feeling of low self-worth often accompany the act of procrastination. Our very inaction is an act. It's deciding not to decide, which can often lead us down a treacherous road. If you're a breathing human being, you've been affected by procrastination to some degree: the late fee at the library for overdue books, the surcharge for overnight delivery because you pushed off sending that birthday gift for too long after you bought it, the sour look on your editor's face when you're past deadline—again. Despite our bad experiences, we continue to push the envelope, addressed to no one other than ourselves.

To illustrate optimum versus procrastinator time lines, take a look at the graph on the following page.

Students are particularly notorious for waiting until the last minute to accomplish their work. If you have ever pulled an all-nighter in college, you will know the feeling of getting things done at the very last minute. The average person reaches a plateau of effort over a longer period of time than the procrastinating student. According to this chart, the optimum scenario involves a shorter warm-up time period than average before sustaining the same level of effort until well before deadline.

If it really is uncomfortable to procrastinate, why do so many of us put off things to the last minute? Is it the thrill of

Monitoring effort

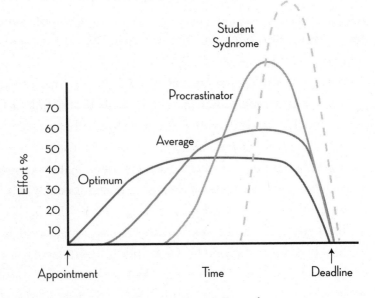

Source: Global Knowledge, www.GlobalKnowledge.com[1]

the adrenaline rush? Is it our desire to test our limits? Or are we simply too stymied by our daily demands to distinguish what's most important? Could it possibly have something to do with our relationship with time?

The answer is: sort of. Being chronically late is a form of procrastination. Burning the midnight oil is another one. All types of procrastination lead to time-sucking activities. But associate professor of psychology Timothy A. Pychyl at Carleton University in Ottawa claims procrastination is a problem of self-regulation, not of understanding time. His research reveals procrastinators understand time very well. The issue lies deeper than just managing your activities. To get to the bottom of procrastination, we have to delve deeper into the phenomenon itself.

Loren Gelberg-Goff is a New Jersey–based licensed clinical social worker who has seen a lot of procrastinators in her twenty-plus years in private practice. She identifies three types of procrastinators: arousal seekers who look for a buzz by pulling things off at the last minute; avoiders who wish to sidestep the fear of failure, then reinforce their fear by not trying; and non-decision makers who have trouble prioritizing and sorting out their lives. According to Loren, procrastination is merely another way of expressing your fear. "Most of the time people have trouble admitting to feeling fear, so they make excuses instead. Procrastination is all about the excuses, whether they're voiced out loud or just race around in our heads."

According to associate professor for human relations and organizational dynamics at the University of Calgary Piers Steel, procrastination makes people fatter, unhappier, and less financially stable. He conducted a meta-analysis of more than five hundred psychological and economic studies to seek out the root causes and subsequent effects of procrastination. What he found debunks the common belief that perfectionists are the biggest procrastinators because of their fear of not being perfect. Contrary to Albert Ellis and William Knaus's now out-of-print book, *Overcoming Procrastination,* in which they make the perfectionist claim, Professor Steel states perfectionists tend to be more productive and want to "get it done" without delay.[2] As a recovering perfectionist, I can attest to that. In fact, this was one of the first chapters I wrote just to prove I wasn't afflicted with procrastination myself!

According to Steel's theory of motivation, chronic procrastinators account for almost 20 percent of the general population, with the exception of students, who have been gauged as experiencing chronic procrastination as high as 50 percent.[3] Task difficulty and individual sensitivity to time delays are strongly related to bouts of procrastination. People who put things off experience so-called preference reversal. That means they may start something, but halfway through they change their minds and never finish it.

Procrastination is widespread and on the rise. Whether you believe perfectionists are procrastinators or not, chances are you have put off something unpleasant at least once in your lifetime. After analyzing more than two hundred studies on procrastination, Professor Steel discovered that more Americans consider themselves procrastinators today than they did three decades ago. While only 5 percent called themselves procrastinators in 1978, 26 percent did so by 2007.[4] It is a noticeable shift in the way people perceive themselves and their relationship with time.

The word "procrastination" stems from the Latin verb *procrastinare*. *Pro* means forward motion while *crastinus* refers to "tomorrow." Procrastination is an expression of denial, stemming from a deep-seated fear of failure and a lack of our own engagement in life. The result is guilt and, at worst, sustained paralysis. Within the context of grief, Timothy Pychyl says, "Procrastination is, quite often, a failure to grasp our own agency in life. It's a life of inauthentic engagement, or lack of engagement, which can bring with it deep regrets of omission."[5] In other words, when we put off taking specific action, we later experience regret for not doing what needed to be done before it was too late. The solution he offers is becoming the authors of our own lives, which we will address more in the principles below.

As Professor Pychyl recommends, we need to replace our sense of urgency and paralysis with a sense of agency and engagement. It's not about feeling bad that we've put things off, but about recognizing those feelings and sorting through them. While some level of procrastination may always be present in our lives, we can learn to work through our blockage and time-sucking activities in simple ways.

Principle #1: Mastering Your Own Ship

Staring at the starlit sky is a humbling experience. You begin to realize how many more energy forms exist beyond Earth, not to mention outside our galaxy. According to scientists, there are billions of galaxies inside the *visible* universe alone. But what lies beyond that? We don't really know. It is easy to feel insignificant when you realize how immeasurably large the universe is. What does it matter if you pay that bill today or tomorrow? The truth is, inside your very own Universe, you are the star. You are the master of your own ship.

You can observe how little control people feel they have over themselves when they come up with excuses as to why, for instance, they simply cannot be on time for appointments. These little white lies become the person's truth, overshadowing their own power and ability to change. Most people resist change because it involves actually thinking about the self-destructive behaviors that got them in the situation in the first place. It's the little voice inside that nudges you in the wrong direction. In German that voice is called *der innere Schweinehund*, literally the "inner pig-dog." It symbolizes the weaker self that gives in to the temptation of procrastination

and inaction. We all have a pig-dog just crying to be fed. Some of us nurture our pig-dog more than others. It feeds off our doubt, our fear and, most important, our time.

When we take responsibility for our lives, a strange thing happens. We unleash a new way of thinking and, with it, an enormous amount of energy and time we used to waste hiding the truth from ourselves. Change takes place almost effortlessly as we realize we have more control than we ever thought imaginable.

Lauren Zander, chairman of the Handel Group, advises people to take charge of their lives by first tackling the withheld and hidden thoughts that are running the show. For instance, regarding our relationships, we often have tacit agreements with our partners. You won't say anything about my inability to resist my daily donut, and I won't say anything about your getting fall-down drunk at parties. Enabling others, instead of empowering them to rise up to their higher selves, leads to codependency and remaining stuck in a rut. Lauren writes: "Identifying your self-truths is where the real work of making change starts—it is crucial to discover what your self-theories are and then to examine why you believe them."[6]

In this exercise, you will need to identify what your self-truths are. Carefully work through the following:

- What hidden things do you tell yourself that don't really serve you, such as "I don't deserve it," "I'm not worth it," "What will people think?" "I'm just not that type of person," "It's genetic," and so on?

- Replace each sentence with a positive statement. For example, "I deserve it," "I'm worth it," "I can do it," "What do I think?" "I embrace who I am."
- Practice your positive affirmations in the mirror or in a voice recorder. Put notes around your living space to remind you of your new commitment to mastering your own ship.
- Hold a symbolic burial for your pig-dog. His ghost may occasionally linger, but you can remove his trapped body from your mind.

Shauna Moerke suffered from chronic procrastination all through middle and high school because she would tell herself she wasn't smart enough. In fact, she almost missed her  college application deadlines because she was so fearful she wouldn't get accepted anywhere. After her first quarter in college, however, she took a class that improved her study skills so much that she landed on the dean's list. Her feeling of success drove her to later complete not only her BA in psychology but also a master's degree.

She chose procrastination as the topic of her thesis in hopes of helping others break through the cycle as she did. She now works as a human resources professional with a particular interest in procrastination in the workplace. Shauna successfully worked through her false self-truths to find her higher purpose. All she needed was to experience the feeling of success to debunk the falsehoods she had been telling herself all along.

Principle #2: Create Your Pockets of Win

Lack of motivation is a primary cause of procrastination. Sometimes we have to trick ourselves into moving forward, in spite of the pig-dog trying to lure us back into his odiferous cage.

To keep on track, create *pockets of win* to coincide with particularly challenging moments in your life. Pockets of win refer to a reward system based on allowing yourself moments in time when you are guaranteed to balance positive emotions against possible negative ones. This helps offset the temptation to fall back into your old ways again, by offering you a yin-and-yang perspective.

If you know you're going to have a tough week, creating pockets of win can be especially helpful to level out the stress you may be experiencing in the moment. For instance, you have a huge project deadline at work, which stresses you out every quarter. Designate a time when you will do something you love, such as watching your favorite movie, to offset the negative feelings you may experience during the big push at the office. If you get a thrill out of selling items on eBay, run an auction during that week to keep your mood upbeat while chaos is swirling around you. These rewards of checking the number of bidders or viewing a good film are not designed to aid your procrastination, but to actually motivate you to continue on even when you'd rather not.

Pockets of win are a self-regulation tool. There's nothing wrong with rewarding yourself when the going gets tough. The point is to keep going once you've gotten started and to not use your rewards to distract, but to congratulate yourself when you've reached your goal.

Celebrating milestones is something Kimberly Richey, a senior sales director for a cosmetics firm, understands well. Working from home, she sees procrastination as her biggest barrier to productivity because there is always something infinitely more interesting to do. She has developed a system of naming each hour so she can readily identify what she will do next. Family hour, spiritual hour, prospects hour, booking appointments hour, and so on are all mapped out for her to help her avoid falling into a black hole of inaction. When she's reached a milestone, she rewards herself by engaging in a fun activity commensurate to the work she has completed. It might be as simple as an ice cream cone with the kids, or a massage after a particularly grueling task. "It is my belief that everyone works better with a carrot dangling before them."

Find your carrot. Create your pockets of win and fill them with rewards. The next thing you'll know, you're moving forward without even realizing it.

Principle #3: Five-Minute Commitment

Experts say making a promise to yourself to focus for five minutes on a somewhat undesirable task can help you break through your own hesitation. After five more minutes, make another promise to spend an additional five minutes. Oftentimes it's merely finding a place to start that causes the most concern.

Business development expert Sian Lindemann used to be what she terms the "world's worst procrastinator" until she realized it was costing her money to not finish what she started.

She took baby steps toward her commitment to end her procrastinating ways by telling herself to make the bed the minute
she got up, place the cap back on the toothpaste tube, and
rinse out the sink after every usage. "Done over the long term,
these basic steps set me in motion. Now I experience an actual
discomfort if I *don't* finish what I've started."

In this exercise, ask yourself what small things you could
do differently to have your day run more smoothly. Perhaps
it's making a cup of coffee instead of standing in line at the
corner java joint. Or you vow to limit your YouTube viewing
to one video per day. These changes should not take more
than five minutes each. As chapter 3 showed, changing your
habits takes commitment and time, so you need to engage in
some goal-setting. Plan out on your calendar what you will
do differently starting today, *not tomorrow*. You will start to
see a measurable difference in the way you feel when you
accomplish tasks based on your new commitment to bringing things to completion. Miraculously, you will also find you
suddenly have more time to spend on the things you love
doing.

List five simple things that take five minutes or less that you
will do differently for thirty days. Record them on your wall
calendar to remind you of your five-minute commitment. It
might not take an entire month for you to expand your activities into other realms of your life. Celebrate your tiny successes
with a gold star on your calendar. If that sounds too childish
for you, reward yourself by dedicating your saved time to an
activity you truly enjoy.

Principle #4: Tackle Hard Stuff Earlier in the Day

We all have different times of day that are our peak performance times. Instead of waiting until the last minute to tackle the less desirable activities, start with them first, when you're at your best.

Chronobiology is the study of time as it impacts the human body. In 2003, sleep researchers at the Center for Chronobiology at the University of Surrey reported on an isolated gene called Period 3 that is responsible for people's sleep preference. Dr. Simon Archer and his team noted that a person's circadian rhythm is deeply impacted by sleep timing and lifestyle.[7]

Whether you are a morning person or a night owl, this preference appears to be partly genetic. According to these scientists, lifestyle is also a deciding factor for up to 80 percent of the population, so it is a teachable skill to get up early or stay up late as long as you get the sleep you need. Any nursing mother of newborn twins can tell you how adaptable you can be when duty calls.

Chronopsychology is a sister discipline involving the scientific study of changes in our daily sleep-wake cycles as it adversely impacts our ability to work well. Shift workers and transmeridian workers such as flight attendants and airline pilots are notorious examples. Perhaps the most astounding discovery about time perception and sleep-wake cycles was made almost five decades ago. In 1962, French caver and geologist Michael Siffre spent 205 days in a subterranean cave while measuring glacier activities. Simultaneously, he conducted a chronopsychological experiment in which he relied solely on his internal clock. The only direct line he had was to his team of researchers above ground. He would phone up to his colleagues, telling them what time he would go to bed or wake up, which they carefully logged. After over two months, he exited the cave thinking the experiment had been terminated early. He was surprised to learn that six times as many days had passed than he thought. Obviously, light plays a large part in determining our sleep-wake cycle and strongly informs our time perception.

You don't need to sleep in an underground cave to determine when you are most productive. Most likely, you already know. Work through the blockage by committing the first part of your day to getting one "hard" thing done. Many people have found that what seemed hard before they started wasn't nearly as hard as the self-flagellation they engaged in before attempting the project in the first place.

Principle #5: Abandon Limbo Through Words

Most of our stress comes from a sense of urgency that we aren't doing what we need to do fast enough. So, instead of doing something, we put off doing anything at all. Couple your feeling of urgency with not making a decision, and you've got a bad case of nerves. It's like going 100 mph in first gear. It's a bad idea.

At the core of many interpersonal conflicts is a breakdown in communication. We put off actually asking questions for fear of rejection or, worse, getting fired on the spot. Without a shared reality between people, conflict is bound to occur. We harbor negative emotions, fretting about what only exists in our heads. Soon we are paralyzed, making matters even worse.

In this case, effective communication is the tool to liberate yourself from the shackles of negative emotions and time-wasting concerns. Take the communication challenge by addressing something you may be fearful to share with someone else. Perhaps it's a cube mate who speaks too loudly on the phone. Or maybe you need to address an issue with your neighbor that's long been bothering you.

As we discussed in chapter 4, acknowledging the person with whom you have the conflict can be extremely powerful. For instance, your boss transfers his anxiety about not making deadline onto you by creating a set of impossible demands. Acknowledge your boss's desire to get it all done now, then lay out a plan for him on how you will tackle each step. If he presents competing priorities, bring it up. "I see that you need the spreadsheet by 4 P.M. Would you like me to table the diagram due at 3 P.M. to complete that or shall I ask Candice to take on the diagram project while we work toward the 4 P.M. deadline?" Addressing the issue head-on is often better, and a sure antidote to procrastination. If you put off clearing up misunderstandings, you will only plant more seeds of possible conflict.

Powerful communication is only possible after you become clear in your own mind what the conflict you're avoiding might be. Raise your own awareness first by considering the situation. Can you ever remember a time when finger-pointing led to a peaceful resolution? Most likely, you cannot. The second step is raising the awareness in others about the dilemma at hand. Giving your conflict partner a so-called reality check (without malice) can help considerably.

Productive, thus positive, stress comes when you identify a

problem and take steps to correct it. Procrastinators are notorious for letting things slide and avoiding conflict. Whether they are in a bad relationship, challenged by their children's behavior, overworked by a tyrannical boss, or steeped in crisis with an aging parent, people often tend to feel they should be able to handle it all. As a result, they often overwork themselves without the productivity positive stress can bring. Women are particularly susceptible to the do-it-all syndrome.* The truth is women are programmed by society to nurture without limits. As a result, we often run ourselves into the ground.

No matter our gender, the key is to retrain our minds to understand there are limits to what we can, and should, do. Create a network of people to support you. Hire a babysitter at set times during your week to eliminate unnecessary stress. Check your superhero cape at the door. This is your life we're talking about!

As Principle #1 shows, our lives are in our own hands and no one else's. Taking personal responsibility for our attitudes and actions can free us to shape our lives the way we want. Stress can be the tool we use occasionally to raise our awareness about what's truly important.

Principle #6: Just Do It

Thinking is an important aspect of the power of slow. But sometimes we overthink things to the degree that we completely paralyze ourselves. What would your life look like if you delved into something *without* thinking? Before you feel

---

*In a 2007 Sleep in America poll conducted by the National Sleep Foundation, 60 percent of the thousand women surveyed sacrificed one or more nights of sleep to get it all done. http://pub.ucsf.edu/newsservices/releases/200703052/.

the tickle in the back of your neck that precedes your deluge of excuses, pause for a moment. If you struggle with completing things or painfully drawing them out, why not shut out the voice of "reason" and just do it. The only thing you really have to lose are the excuses themselves.

Start small. We're not talking about rearranging your entire house, cleaning your attic, filing your taxes on January 2, or losing ten pounds in a week. If you've been staring at that pile of clothes for three weeks, pick off one item a day until it is gone. Put "just do it" stickers in your calendar, on your car steering wheel, or even your bathroom mirror.

Master coach Peter Pamela Rose admits the feeling of procrastination is worse than the thing she actually fears doing. "I honestly hate the feeling of having to get something done more than getting the actual thing I need to get done completed!" She attributes her "just do it" mentality to discipline, a skill she has taken years to develop and that is now one of the core traits she coaches people to master. "Once you have mastered discipline," she states, "you can accomplish *anything*."

Barbara Hemphill, who has been involved in personal productivity for over three decades, grappled with procrastination for years. It often left her deeply depressed until one day she started therapeutic treatment to deal with her issues around putting things off. During a particularly challenging art therapy session, her instructor gave her the permission to draw something really ugly. She started slowly, feeling the buildup until she finally unleashed her creative flow. In that moment, she had an epiphany about what had held her back all these years. "I realized that my procrastination was a result of fear—the fear of being less than perfect, fear of failing, the fear of mak-

ing a mistake, the fear of being rejected. That experience re-
sulted in a totally new life adventure for me. Now I *just do it*
instead of thinking about it and then beating myself up because I didn't at least try." She asks herself two simple questions: "What?" and "When?" "I ask: 1) What is the *next* action I
need to take to accomplish this task? Sometimes a task involves several steps—but you can only do them one at a time!
and 2) When? Then I put a reminder in my file folder system
with designated months that sits on my desk." Barbara got
a handle on her lethargy by breaking her tasks down into
smaller steps. She no longer listens to the excuses that used to
haunt her.

Principle #7: File Your Taxes, Not Your Nails

Dolly Parton's character, the buxom nail-filing secretary, in the
1980 movie *Nine to Five* should be your visual. Imagine yourself,
like Dolly, filing your nails instead of all the documents sitting
atop your desk. She never got in any real trouble for gossiping
and wasting time at work or even for binding and gagging her
discriminatory boss. But that's Hollywood. The IRS is a little less
forgiving.

According to a 2007 H&R Block consumer survey, 53 percent of all tax filers planned on waiting until March or April
to file their taxes. Among those surveyed, 11 percent were split
almost equally among three excuses as to why they couldn't
yet file: "too busy," "afraid they owed the IRS money," and simply "procrastinating."[8] Professor Steel found the average tax de-
linquent paid an extra four hundred dollars due to last-minute
filing, rushing, and the resulting errors.[9]

Certified professional organizer Susan Fox converts her clients to online banking as a powerful solution to keeping on top of their financial records. Not everyone is comfortable with the idea, so she also suggests automating people's systems in a more conventional way by designating a specific day to pay the bills. It is also important to sort through the mail in the same spot every time. The best thing is to have a container that you can stand over every time you retrieve the mail to eliminate unnecessary papers right away.

"Often, when I conduct an assessment, my procrastinating clients have no systems in place. They pile mail (unopened), junk mail included, into boxes and containers. They have no assigned days to sit down and pay bills," Susan told me. "Setting up a specific location in the home where mail is taken to be reviewed, and having a system for recycling, shredding, or retaining all in one place helps. However, having a blocked out, calendared time is the most important thing to assure that clients actually make the time to do this work."

Whatever your situation, this exercise has you take inventory of your system. Ask yourself if you have a functional routine in place to deal with important documents, tax-related receipts, bills, and the like. If you do not, consider starting a filing system for papers as they come in. If you are self-employed, regularly clear out your wallet or purse for receipts you can later document as business expenses. Label envelopes with specific headings such as "client meals," "transportation," and "marketing." Keep them together in one binder or folder. At year's end, consider the act of doing your taxes as an opportunity to enjoy your entire year in review. It may be an unusual approach, but doing your taxes can be a lot like scrapbooking.

It gives you an opportunity to remember what you've done over the course of the year.

If you don't like doing the tax paperwork yourself, hire someone else to do it for you. But remember to ask for help in advance of the mid-April deadline.

Principle #8: Involve Other People

Nothing will make you get something done more readily than if you tell the world what you're about to do. There's a heightened sense of culpability when others are aware of your plans. If you have trouble keeping yourself accountable to do what you say you're going to do, tell someone in your life who scares you just a little. Whether that's an older sibling, a parent, or a mentor, telling someone you deeply respect will make you feel more accountable to actually act on it. Suddenly, you've put your butt on the line.

Practical marketing expert Stacy Karacostas suggests telling other people your goals as a way to combat procrastination. "Knowing that you've publicly declared you're going to do something makes you far more likely to do it." Just the idea of having to face the embarrassment of other people knowing you didn't do it can keep you plowing forward.

Putting yourself in the place of no return might sound scary, but if you suffer from chronic procrastination, it's the very thing that will motivate you.

When Mary Parker was a full-time U.S. Marine attending school part time, she learned the importance of holding herself accountable for doing her work after failing her first class, which led to her having to reimburse the military 100 percent for the course tuition. Apart from the financial pain, she learned the biggest lesson of all: Procrastination never pays. Taking accelerated classes meant she could get behind in less time if she slacked off again. It was a big commitment to overcome procrastination, but she soon learned she had no way around doing the work. Taking on the military would have been worse than actually doing the assignments themselves. She was accountable to a very large organization as well as to herself to complete her assignments on time. After failing that first class, she learned to reward herself by doing something fun only *after* she had completed her homework each night. By creating a tight structure she couldn't wriggle out of, Mary was able to finish the program successfully. She now serves as a lieutenant commander in the the U.S. Navy.

Principle #9: Maintain Your Momentum By Breaking Things into Parts

The business world is full of great examples of the negative impact procrastination can have on employees and business owners alike. For instance, many business owners struggle with the fourth-quarter woes. They don't stick to their time line, so they end the year with a final race to the finish. Maintaining your momentum throughout the year keeps you balanced. If you don't pay attention to the little things that you dropped along the way, their impact grows exponentially as the year unfolds. Allowing lint to accumulate on your wheel axle will eventually bring the whole wagon to a halt.

As we have seen, procrastinating costs not only peace of mind but also money. Business owners experience the price of

procrastination firsthand. Insurance agency owner and professional speaker Laura Harris learned a valuable lesson after spending several years doing the year-end push. By December of
every year, her team members were as exhausted as she was.

"At the end of the year there was always a tremendous
push to do the last-minute things necessary to make sure we
achieved our annual goals," said Laura. "The fourth quarter was
one big 'catch up' in the areas where we were not on pace.
January brought the inevitable stress of having to start from
scratch again. It was like climbing a mountain only to see you
hit ground zero the very next month." One day she met a busi-
nessman who didn't seem to have this problem. He maintained
his momentum consistently throughout the twelve months. Asking him his secret, Laura learned he was committed to having
four good quarters. In January, he would set his annual goals. At
the end of each quarter, he would evaluate his company's performance to see if they were on track. If something got dropped,
he would pick it up right away, tweaking his course where
needed. Avoiding the snowball effect, he maintained his momentum by treating each set of three months as if it had an end
goal itself. The key to moving forward was simply breaking
down the year to match his business activities with his goals.
"His insight helped me realize that just having measurements
was not enough," admitted Laura. "If we were not on pace for
our annual goals, we could not afford to procrastinate. The longer we waited, the more difficult corrections became. Now our
goal is to have four good quarters. December is just another
month. We no longer panic at the end of the year and no longer
get depressed at the beginning of the year either."

Evaluate how you operate throughout the year. Consider

breaking up your year into manageable parts to make all twelve months more even-keeled. It's all about developing strategies the way Laura did to ensure a smoother ride.

Principle #10: Save the Best for Last

Children offer a marvelous opportunity for looking at what happens before things go terribly wrong for us as adults. Each young life is like a clean slate with seemingly endless possibilities of hope. Despite their individual quirks and personalities, a lot of what children do as they get older is learned behavior. They're great reference material, modeling how life could be if we stopped all the negative self-talk and simply did what we need to do without all the forethought and negative emotion.

Approaching the tabula rasa of human beings, I recently asked my children, aged eight and ten, why they insisted on doing their homework the moment they got home from school.

"We love to play with friends so we get the hard stuff out of the way first. We just get it done so we don't have to worry about it anymore," my ten-year-old revealed. There wasn't even a hint of dread, fear, or anxiety in her tone. It was inspiring to see 'just do it' in action.

Self-proclaimed procrastinator Emily Yoffe wrote in an article on Slate.com how she learned the best lesson of all from her twelve-year-old daughter: Save the best for last. Much like my own kids, her daughter does her schoolwork and piano practice faithfully without her mom's nagging. She claims it was something she learned back in preschool. At snack time, she would receive five pieces of popcorn, five gummi bears, and five pretzels. Since she liked the pretzels the most, she saved them to the end while most of her classmates gobbled up their favorite foods first. They were left unhappy, having to eat their least favorite while she savored the flavor of her beloved pretzels at the end. "I realized if I saved [the pretzels] for last, I'd get the taste of them in my mouth the longest," she told her mom.

"So now, if I can get my homework done, then I have the rest of my night to do whatever I want."

In this exercise, identify what your "best" is. Perhaps it is your favorite dessert, a call with your best friend, or a movie  you've been wanting to see for a long time. What flavor do you want to savor the longest? Like Emily Yoffe's daughter, allow that feeling to linger by keeping it for the end of your day, week, or month. Make it your golden promise to yourself. It is the reward you have earned for slaying the pigdog once and for all.

Final Word

Procrastination is a slippery slope that hinders you from living the life you deserve. It costs you more than time and money; you lose your sense of well-being, too. This chapter encouraged you to be the master of your own ship, create your pockets of win, make a five-minute commitment to difficult tasks, work on harder tasks earlier in the day, take personal responsibility through effective communication, just do it, design a filing system to meet important deadlines, hold yourself accountable by telling other people of your plans, take baby steps, and re-member what you learned in preschool by saving the best for last. Once you've implemented these strategies, you are now in a position to spend the free time you've earned to do what you truly love. You are now starting to reclaim your personal bank account of time. How you spend its contents is entirely up to you.

In the next chapter, we will address what to do with the free time you have and how easy it is to find it if you look.

6

Free Time Is Not Expensive. It's, Well, Free!: Ten Ways to Do What You Love

Cathy Thorne © www.everyday people cartoons.com

I ONLY HAVE 2 SPEEDS: SPEED OF LIGHT,
AND SPEED OF LUMP.

> Time is all you have. And you may find one day that you have
> less than you think.
>
> —Randy Pausch (1960–2008)[1]

After working thirty days straight, Shel Horowitz, author of *Principled Profit*, peeled himself from his chair for a little rest and relaxation in Vermont. It wasn't until after he had dragged himself away from his typewriter (it was 1982, after all) that he realized how much he had needed to get away. From that point onward, he made a few rules of conduct for himself: no client work on weekends and plenty of vacation time. He devised strategies to draw on whenever he felt himself get off kilter: a bike ride, a visit to the theater, or a long weekend with his wife. While he doesn't always achieve the necessary balance, he has become more mindful of how he spends his time. "These small steps have helped me find the truly visionary ideas that I express in my work as an author." Valuing his free time with friends and family as much as his work time, Shel has melded both by choosing a life he loves.

Somewhere along the line, a lot of us have made decisions leading up to our overworked and underplayed lives. Leisure time, *Time* magazine's Nancy Gibbs commented in 1989, has become an expensive commodity. In a phone interview with Penn State University professor emeritus of leisure studies Geoffrey Godbey, I learned Americans have an average of thirty-five hours of leisure time per week during weekdays, with fewer hours of free time on the weekends due to household chores, grocery shopping, and other errands. It's an astounding number, given how time-crunched many of us feel. A workweek contains 120 hours. After you subtract an assumed forty-five hours for working and commuting along with Godbey's thirty-five hours of leisure time, we still have forty hours of sleep and eating time left. We have more time than we think, yet take a look at what we do with the free time we have.

Not surprisingly, the majority of leisure time is spent in front of the television. Godbey's conclusion is *not* that all Americans are couch potatoes, but that their leisure time is bite-sized, even during the week. It is the duration of singular free moments that impact the activities Americans choose to do. According to

Godbey, you can't play a round of golf in thirty minutes, but you can catch a rerun of your favorite sitcom in that time. He claims golf is not a booming industry amongst the wider population. Why? Because it takes too long. The minute increments of free time spanning the thirty-five hours during the week explain why television consumption is such a common leisure activity. It's all the time people have in that moment.

In our 24/7 world, weekend leisure time has been squeezed considerably. Stores are open seven days a week; some are open twenty-four hours a day. Sunday is no longer seen as a day of rest, but as a day to do laundry, grocery shop, and pay the bills. In the film *Thank You for Smoking*, tobacco lobbyist Nick Naylor gets a late-night phone call from an L.A. producer. When asked why he's still in the office, the producer says it is 4 P.M. the next day in Japan. Before the producer clicks off to take another call, this time from London, Nick presses him further to ask when he ever sleeps. The producer replies: "Sunday." His response is a play on the classical notion of Sunday as a day of rest. Ironically, it is also the character's *only* day in which he sleeps at all. This scene reveals a common reality about globalization. While we sleep, it is late tomorrow on the other side of the planet. Many of us feel compelled to adapt to other countries' time zones just to keep up, even if it means doing business in the middle of the night. Our time perception shifts, as does the definition of "regular working hours." This distortion of time upends our circadian rhythm, leaving us feeling time-starved and exhausted.

From a historical perspective, the pace of our lives has continued to increase. While Nancy Gibbs bemoaned the age of fax machines in the late '80s, a new generation deals with the instantaneous nature of digital communication. With constant availability, the lines between leisure and work have undeniably blurred. In fact, the public domain is no longer treated as it once was: a place in which social skills rule. Trapped on a forty-five-minute shuttle bus ride from JFK airport to downtown Manhattan, an entire group of people, including myself, listened to a boisterous one-way conversation a visitor from Singapore was having with her sister back home. People chatting loudly on their cell phones with loved ones on public transportation is evidence of the growing trend of privacy made public. While many of us internally asked ourselves if her call could have waited, in a life informed by speed, waiting is unthinkable. We make private phone calls a part of the public domain simply *because we can.*

Not only our everyday lives but also scientific exploration has taken on a whole new temporal gravity. An international team of scientists in Geneva, Switzerland, have begun swirling atoms in opposing directions with such velocity that they hope to simulate the conditions associated with the collision believed to have led to the Big Bang. News reports hype up the possibility of the world being swallowed into a black hole as the speed demons we are peer into the vortex with a blend of thrill and fear.

Closer to home, our time-saving household gadgets, once praised as devices untethering housewives from time-robbing chores, have clogged our countertops while leaving us with no more time than before. Our schedules have reached a new level of ambition as we pile more and more things on our to-do list, crowding out downtime altogether. In the minds of many, free time is considered a guilty pleasure reserved for the lazy or filthy rich. Jeremy Rifkin, in *Time Wars*, claims, "It is ironic that in a culture so committed to saving time we feel increasingly deprived of the very thing we value."[2]

According to a 2008 Leisure Trends Group poll, 57 percent of Americans believe life is too short to spend it all at work.[3] Generation X is a particularly conflicted demographic. While they hold the belief that life is about more than work, they are the group most likely to give up weekends and vacation time for the office. Only 39 percent stated flexibility of work time was a key factor in determining whether they would stay with a company longer. Clearly, our actions are not in alignment with our beliefs.

It is apparent from this survey and others that people value free time, yet too few actually take it. In *The Now Habit*, Neil Fiore recommends guilt-free play as a way of actually ending time-wasting activities. Recreation, after all, is about re-creating our sense of joy. The most productive people are those who have matched their fun with their duty. They view life as a give and take. They must *take* time for themselves in order to *give* back at the workplace. Given Americans' commitment to productivity and efficiency, it appears to be an easy enough formula for success. But if the formula is so simple, why don't more people take time off?

According to a poll conducted by the National Recreation and Park Association, 38 percent of those surveyed reported that they "always felt rushed." A similar number was reported among Canadians as well.[4] The sense of urgency we've discussed in previous chapters pervades almost every aspect of our lives. Free time, the antithesis of the rush-rush lifestyle, has no place in a world made up of work and production. Fiore explores the link between chronic procrastinators and workaholics. Neither is more productive than those who take time off, because they lack a sense of guilt-free play. Ironically, leisure is a key component to efficiency.

Even when we do take time off, our leisure activities often mirror our love of speed. Jam-packed with visits from one place to the next, our vacations often bring to mind the old saying of "It's Tuesday, this must be Belgium," without allowing us to absorb much of anything other than possibly jet fuel or bus fumes. Some of us seek out extreme conditions to spike our adrenaline levels even higher. A rising trend in adventure vacations proves there is an increasing number of people seeking to fill their free time with more dangerous, adrenaline-soaking activities such as skydiving, mountain marathons, glacier climbing, and spelunking. We ignore the power of slow, returning exhilarated, but possibly also exhausted from the blur and rush experience.

What I am advocating here is not bungee-jumping over the Grand Canyon or scaling down a skyscraper but an occasional slower approach to your well-earned leisure. Have you ever wondered why you get your best ideas in the shower or on the golf course? As you switch off your conscious mind, the wheels of your subconscious mind continue to turn. Relaxation sets in, engaging your subconscious mind to mull over ideas almost effortlessly. Leisure time literally frees up your thoughts to give you more rapid solutions than merely pounding the keyboard, staring at a ledger sheet, or peering at a blank canvas for hours on end will yield.

The quickened pace of our lives over the past decade can be seen in numbers. In 1997, Dr. Robert Levine at California State University combined three indicators to measure the pace of life in thirty-one countries: public clock accuracy, pedestrian speed, and post office speed. One was the fastest; thirty-one the slowest. Perhaps unsurprisingly, Switzerland ranked first, with Ireland coming in second, and Germany third. Singapore ranked fifteenth.

Dr. Richard Wiseman, professor of psychology at the University of Hertfordshire, led a follow-up study in 2007 that singularly clocked urban dwellers' pace by measuring how long, on average, it took them to walk sixty feet. The fastest pedestrians were in Singapore; the slowest in the thirty-two countries studied were in Blantyre, Malawi. As figure 1 reveals, a fast pace of life is not reserved only for Western nations. The Bernese in Switzerland, for instance, ranked number thirty in Dr. Wiseman's research, dethroning Switzerland from its first-place ranking just a decade ago. Dr. Levine's original study, as reported in his book *A Geography of Time* in 1997, showed the average pace to be slower *overall* among the top-ranked city dwellers as compared to 2007. Based on these indicators, the general pace of life worldwide has indeed gotten faster. As an example, Singaporeans move 30 percent quicker than they did just ten years ago. Dr. Wiseman points to the more frequent use of high-speed technology as the main culprit for our urgency.

How Fast Is Your City?

Average time taken (in secs) to walk 60ft

Fastest	Secs
1. Singapore (Singapore)	10.55:
2. Coppenhagen (Denmark)	10.82:
3. Madrid (Spain)	10.89:
4. Guangzhou (China)	10.94:
5. Dublin (Ireland)	11.03:
6. Curitiba (Brazil)	11.13:
7. Berlin (Germany)	11.16:
8. New York (USA)	12.00:
9. Utrecht (Netherlands)	12.04:
10. Vienna (Austria)	12.06:
11. Warsaw (Poland)	12.07:
12. London (United Kingdom)	12.17:
13. Zagreb (Croatia)	12.20:
14. Prague (Czech Republic)	12.35:
15. Wellington (New Zealand)	12.62:
16. Paris (France)	12.65:
17. Stockholm (Sweden)	12.75:
18. Ljubljana (Slovenia)	12.76:
19. Tokyo (Japan)	12.83:
20. Ottawa (Canada)	13.72:
21. Harare (Zimbabwe)	13.92:
22. Sofia (Bulgaria)	13.96:
23. Taipei (Taiwan)	14.00:
24. Cairo (Egypt)	14.18:
25. San'a (Yemen)	14.29:

26.	Bucharest (Romania)	14.36:
27.	Dubai (United Arab Emirates)	14.64:
28.	Damascus (Syria)	14.94:
29.	Amman (Jordan)	15.95:
30.	Bern (Switzerland)	17.37:
31.	Manama (Bahrain)	17.69:
32.	Blantyre (Malawi)	31.60:
	Slowest	

Source: Richard Wiseman's project Web site www.paceoflife.co.uk

Time perception can have a significant impact on well-being. For instance, in a quality of life study by the General Social Survey drawing on data collected for thirty-four years with forty-five thousand participants, sociologists John P. Robinson and Steven Martin at the University of Maryland reported that 35 percent of all unhappy people always felt rushed for time compared to 23 percent who stated they were "very happy."[5] The study found television viewing was most frequent in unhappy people, indicating that TV consumption overall has no lasting benefit. Clearly, what we do with our time has a long-term effect on our level of happiness. Unhappy people feel more rushed, yet watch more TV than happy people. A minor shift in what they do (in this case, watching less TV) might alter the number of unhappy people significantly.

Given these numbers, it is no wonder our free time feels so expensive. But Aesop's fable of the tortoise and the hare reminds us that speed does not always serve us best. In fact, sometimes being slow brings us to the finish line faster.

*   *   *

This chapter will delve into ways you can remind yourself of the importance of leisure time. While Godbey and others make the distinction between free time and leisure, we will use these terms interchangeably. The select principles have been designed for you to ease your way into the idea that incorporating moments of leisure into your life will not result in the proverbial sky falling. In fact, afterward you may find yourself packing your bags, and this book along with them.

Principle #1: Flip-Flop Walk*

You know the sound you make when you wear flip-flops. It's the rhythmic sound of summer, a veritable metronome of leisure. If you've ever tried to run in flip-flops, you know it's not a good idea. Flip without the flop will land you on your nose. The flip is the yin to the flop's yang. They belong in harmony. Flip-flops audibly smack of slow, and they are the best tools for reducing your pace, if even a little.

For the purposes of this exercise, you must wear flip-flops, so you'll need to dig out your summer footwear. If you don't own a pair, get some. Once you've secured your summer shoes, walk around your living space. Note the sound you make as you walk. How fast are you going? Use a stopwatch to see how fast you go from your car to the store, for instance. If the weather allows, wear them while running errands, although in this case, due to your footwear, you'll be walking them. How do they sound now as you beat the pavement?

*To get the best overview of your own pace of life, this mindfulness exercise is best done when it is warm outside.

Where do you speed up? At the mall? The grocery store?
Where do you flip-flop more slowly? At the bookstore? The
hair salon? Are you more likely to walk fast during the week or
on the weekend?

In a journal, make one fast column and one slow column.
Record the places where you walked faster or slower in the appropriate columns. Highlight the areas where you walked fastest. Make comments as to why you thought you had to go fast.
Perhaps there was a lot of traffic or the area was crowded.

Next, ask someone to measure how quickly you walk sixty
feet when you aren't looking. Where does your pace fall on
the list? In general, are you more of a Singaporean or a Bernese walker? Invite your friends to try it out, too.

Principle #2: Redefine Purpose of Leisure

We often struggle with the idea of spending our free time doing things for the simple pleasure of doing them. We somehow
have grown to believe pleasurable activities serve no higher
purpose. Being purposeful means you are accomplishing tangible things you can later show as the proof of your labor. It's
as if we need permission to engage in leisure activities to remain the productive human beings we claim ourselves to be.
So here's your chance. Give yourself permission by redefining
the purpose of the activity altogether.

Human beings naturally seek meaning in things. It's what
helps us make sense of our world. When something has no
meaning, we place no value on it. Yet leisure time is a highly
valuable aspect of our lives. We have more of it than we think,
yet our sense of leisure has been diminished by the activities

in which we typically engage. Anyone who has spent five hours in front of a television screen will tell you how empty the sensation of time wasted feels.

In this exercise, you have the opportunity to reexamine how you spend your free time, if you do at all. Ask yourself "What's the point?" of doing what you do. We all need to feel a sense of purpose in our actions. Many times we think there is no purpose to spending our leisure time doing fun things we enjoy. It is time to rethink this and allow yourself the downtime you deserve.

Maybe you feel guilty about spending an hour at the gym when you could be reading to your kids at night. Or perhaps you can't quite justify taking that weekend trip with your friends because your partner's not invited. At the same time, you know it would do you a world of good to engage in the activity. Respite is undervalued in a society built on productivity, yet it is the very thing that makes us so productive when we allow ourselves to log off.

In a world that makes you whisper the word "vacation," and then only to your most trusted circle, be a renegade. Understand that in your leisure time, you are contributing equally to the bottom line. You are filling up your tank as you unload the burden and stress of your day-to-day life, clearing the path for new ideas and your higher purpose, too.

Principle #3: List What You Love

Not surprisingly, many of us spend a majority of our time doing what we *have* to do, not what we'd *like* to do. If you are truly honest with yourself, chances are you will have to admit you are among those who are miserly with themselves. Our free time is there for us to enjoy, yet even then we find reasons why we can't pursue what we love to do.

In this exercise, list ten things you love to do. It could look something like the following:

1. Square dancing
2. Riding
3. Sailing
4. Pottery
5. Singing
6. Writing
7. Sewing
8. Cartwheels
9. Stamp Collecting
10. Racing

Now list the reasons you tell yourself why you cannot do each activity, such as:

1. No time
2. Too expensive
3. Can't find a babysitter
4. Don't know where to start
5. It's not important
6. I'm not worth it
7. Somebody's better than me
8. Who cares
9. It's stupid to be so extravagant
10. I can't

The number one reason most people forgo their favored pursuits is closely related to their relationship with time. It harks back to a commonly held time-starved mentality, but the reality is far different. *It is a matter of taking the time you do have and doing what you love.* How? Let's take sewing as an example. You would love to sew a set of curtains for the living room. You even have the sewing machine, which has been in a box, unopened, for five years. The prospect of actually sitting down to complete the entire project sends you reeling. It's easier to say you don't have the time than to admit you have a specific expectation of how the project should go.

To get to the bottom of it, fill in the blanks.

I simply cannot _____ because I expect _____.
For instance, I simply cannot <u>sew the curtains</u> because I expect <u>to finish it all at once</u>.

This statement identifies what is stopping you. Once you have made this realization, you can move to the next step of the process. You have learned you have impossible expectations that will set you up for failure. To avoid failure, you decide not to start at all. By examining your expectation, you can now adjust it to a more realistic goal.

I can _____ because I expect _____.
For instance, I can <u>sew my curtains</u> because I expect <u>to finish them when I am ready</u>.

Knowing you have lowered your expectations to a manageable level, you are now free to break down the project into sizable chunks to pursue what you'd like in the time that you have.

Principle #4: Benefit Versus Burden

At what point does your free time become a burden? It is a modern-day question because we have more free time than we've ever had before. With the regulated forty-hour work-week, many of us enjoy unprecedented amounts of leisure. Before labor laws cracked down on employers, workers were required to work long hours, even on Saturdays. If you look at labor history, however, it seems to go in cycles. We've gone from shorter hours during agrarian times to longer work hours during industrialization to shorter work hours in the post-industrial era to longer work hours as our information society becomes a 24/7 service-based one. Technology allows the tendrils of work to hook us even on our days off.

On numerous occasions I have witnessed people's panic as they handle whatever their BlackBerry is telling them to do during so-called leisure time. The increased accessibility makes time off a burdensome event as they bear witness to what they're supposedly missing. In fact, they aren't missing anything at all. They're simply reinforcing the guilt they felt when they entertained the idea of unplugging for a day. As work and play become one, the benefits of leisure become less and less clear.

In 1930 W. K. Kellogg introduced the six-hour workday in his Battle Creek cereal factory. With a minimal pay cut, he announced that shorter working hours would inspire his fac-

tory workers to work harder. According to Benjamin Hunnicutt's book *Kellogg's Six-Hour Work Day*, it was an immensely
successful experiment that lasted for decades. It instilled a
sense of loyalty and trust in the workers, who appreciated the
extra free time to spend with family. It was a historical example
of work-life balance.

If we are honest, many of us love our work. We are inspired
by what we do for a living and, in many ways, we live to work.
We are so wrapped up in our productivity that it is often unthinkable to unhinge ourselves for even a moment. We ask ourselves how we could possibly take time off from something we
love doing. It almost feels like betrayal.

It is not uncommon to think we might be better off by con-
tinuing to do what we do rather than to disengage. Yet burnout syndrome is evidence of our own undoing when we
do too much. Indeed, too much of a good thing can be harmful, too.

In this exercise, list the pros and cons of taking some time
off. It could simply be a long weekend or an entire week in
which you focus on something outside of your daily routine.
Be honest with yourself as you go down the list. What things
do you tell yourself about taking time off? Do you consider it
a burden or a benefit? Why or why not?

Befriending your leisure time is a significant step in befriending the concept of time altogether. As you allow yourself
some downtime, you will begin to see how the quality of your
life increases dramatically. It doesn't take much, but it does take
something. Most important, it takes confidence and a willingness to let go.

Principle #5: The Absence Test

After those rare moments of getting unplugged, you realize once you return to your daily routine that the sun still rose and set, the office hummed along beautifully, your children still got to school on time, and your house was in one piece when you returned. Your in-box was easily handled after an hour or two of concentrated work, and you wonder why you hadn't thought to take time out long before you actually did.

If you are grappling with the concept of taking time off, you can easily prove to yourself that putting your life on hold for a day won't kill anyone.

To take the absence test, you need a little preparation. Look at your calendar for the next upcoming holiday. It is better to ease yourself into the notion of free time if you do this exercise during a less busy season. The day before or after the holiday, commit to unplugging by not checking your voice mail or e-mails. Pick one or two things you routinely do and omit them from your day. The explanation that others may have is that you were simply out of the office, which is exactly what you will want them to think. The absence test proves to you and to others that not being available 24/7 or even for a day is normal. It also shows that the earth keeps spinning even when you are digitally out of pocket.

Principle #6: Open-Ended Events

We often wonder why time flies when we're having fun. Our time perception becomes skewed because our mind is concentrating on the present moment, such as when we are engrossed in a really good three-hour film that feels only a minute long. We experience a sense of timelessness when we are on vacation, no longer subjected to the rigors of the clock. We ignore the external minutes ticking away, concentrating only on our internal experience. We feel suspended from time or at least oriented toward a different sense of it. In fact, we identify with the events happening around us with such intensity that we forget the clock altogether.

According to anthropologists, there are essentially two types of time orientation: clock time and event time. In much of the world, we orient ourselves toward the clock, which tells us what time we need to rise in the morning, catch the commuter train, or cook an evening meal. On the other hand, events-based time refers to our orientation to certain periodic happenings throughout the year. It is a looser understanding of the time passing that allows for less rigidity in daily planning. Dr. Robert Levine references ethnosociologist Sir Edmund Ronald Leach's work with the Kachin people of North Burma. They have various words to describe the duration of things without any tangible relationship to clock time. *Na* means a long time, *tawng* a short time. *Ta* relates to springtime while *asak* refers to the time within a person's life. Much like Hopi Native Americans, the Kachin people treat their temporal words like adverbs instead of nouns.[6] They look at *how* things, not *which* things, transpire.

This exercise suggests you bring more events-based time perception into your life to ease the burden of clock-induced urgency. As leadership coach Brian Biro remarks, "Open-ended

gives you some nice choice. If the event is wonderful and
filled with connection—stay! If not, then you can look at
open-ended as 'when you decide-ended'!" If you've ever thought
about when you have the most fun at social events, it is typically
when you are not bound by the clock to stay or leave at an appointed hour. Open-ended events allow for a more free-flowing
sense of time.

Another way to approach a more events-based reality is to
decide spontaneously to take a road trip for a day. Perhaps
you have always wanted to visit those waterfalls an hour
away or a new amusement park that opened up near you, but
you could never seem to squeeze an opportunity into your
calendar. Brainstorm about a few places you've wanted to
visit for a while, but haven't because you've defined your life
by the clock instead of events you know would be nurturing
to you.

If the weather permits, jump in your car and go. Stay for as
long as you feel like it instead of imposing a set day and time for
the event. We often think we won't get our money's worth if we
only go to a museum for an hour or leave a movie early if we
don't like it. In our 24/7 world, we live in the "should" of things
instead of basing our actions on our true desires. An events-
based reality helps us decide the organic beginning and ending
of things. Maybe the birthday party is over when the cake is
gone or our mourning period is over when we no longer cry
every day. Perhaps it is time to pursue that favorite hobby for an
undefined period of time simply because it feels right. Choose
an event and allow it to unfold. Use your intuition to guide you
to its natural beginning and ending without once looking at
your wristwatch.

Principle #7: The Art of Hanging Out

"Want to play a game?" My bright-eyed friend whom I hadn't seen in almost a decade sat up straight in her chair. I was passing through her area for two hours and was looking forward to chatting with her about her life in the last ten years. It wasn't how I wanted to spend my time with her. Sorting through her stack of board games, she had clearly not yet mastered the art of hanging out.

Activity is a highly prized notion in our culture. We value "doingness" more than "beingness." Many great books have been written on the importance of being. Eckhardt Tolle's *The Power of Now* addresses the here and now as the only thing we have. So why do we feel so driven to play games with old friends we haven't seen in years instead of just being together? Perhaps our level of comfort is diminished if we aren't actually accomplishing something quantifiable. It's hard to measure the value of hanging out with friends because our expectations about our own productivity often overshadow the value of the friendship itself. Our urgency is underscored by our intense activity level. But are we really gaining more value by acting this way?

Clock time obsession is not common in every country. Burundi is a fabulous example of a place where people measure time by the rhythm of their cattle. In this Central African nation a vast majority of the population is rural. It's only natural then that they embrace life based on events such as grazing or drinking time, not on the clock. As I sat in my friend's parlor, I was aware of the clock like never before, wishing for a new understanding of time to help me through this awkward moment.

Ten years versus two hours felt long and short at the very same time.

Other "doingness" cultures in the Western world offer a crushing feeling of laziness if you wish to sit over a steaming cup of tea for a nice chat. If you aren't contributing to the GNP at every waking moment, you have a sense of disorientation, or worse, of pending doom. Melinda Day-Harper, a former corporate executive and amateur horse jumper, recognized that her type A personality was putting her at risk. In a constant state of "doingness," she failed to slow down until her high-flying life shook her awake: two emergency plane landings and several spills while jumping over fences made her realize "doing" wasn't enough. "Having the time and freedom to just *be* is very important to me now," she admitted to me via e-mail. "It provides a spiritual rejuvenation that I wouldn't otherwise receive. Peace and serenity are grossly underrated! I've been a classic type-A doer all my life. I've *done* a lot; now it's time to focus more on the *being* part."

When she's not assisting clients on productivity issues, Melinda surrounds herself with nature. A typical day includes a romp among the trees with her four dogs. Animals, she says, have a great way of connecting with our inner selves. They bring you into present time without attachment. They are the best teachers for the art of hanging out.

It's puzzling that our art of hanging out has been lost. At the risk of sounding nostalgic, we used to know how to do it a century ago. By way of example, the Quaker worship services included silent prayer without words, not that sitting on an upright bench in New England is exactly chillin' in the colloquial sense. Nevertheless, it allowed for quietude and communion with others without doing much of anything at all.

Recapturing the art of hanging out might seem new to you. You may have never known what it's like to unjam your packed calendar for some breezy time of nothingness. If it's not new to you, but a rusty memory you can recall with some effort, think back to a time when hanging out was a primary activity.

Organize some hang time for yourself by flopping on your couch without clicking on the television. Flip through your favorite magazine or listen to some music. If you start to feel restless, remember your body craves whatever you consistently feed it. If you are normally in constant motion, your body will feel strange as it rests. Be patient with yourself. The art of hanging out is exactly that—art. Picasso didn't learn his art in a day, and neither will you. The point is to simply get started by recognizing how leisure can be integrated into your life in small ways.

Principle #8: The Rule of Full

Downtime is an essential component in our lives. In the rule of full, the quality of your leisure is actually more important than its quantity. Taking a "me" day is a great way to foster your mental health. Before you raise your arms in protest, consider what Tel Aviv University professor Dov Eden and his colleagues discovered. They studied the effects respite can have on the human condition. After interviewing eight hundred academics from the United States, Israel, and New Zealand who took either a one-semester or one-year sabbatical, they discovered these professionals' stress levels returned at the same rate once they resumed their normal activities as academics who had taken either a week-long or long weekend vacation. That means the *quality* of time off impacts the respite effect of leisure more than the *quantity* of days. In other words, fully unplugging for a few days can have the same recharging quality as taking off a full year.[7]

A Washington, D.C.–area architect says she prefers taking a full day to herself instead of a half day because it usually takes a full hour to unwind from work anyway. "It eats into my off-time if I do it that way. Taking a full vacation day beats taking two half days hands down."

What's the reason for this? It has to do with the rule of full. Many of us play a lot of roles. Some of us transition from one to the next, much as we task-switch, within seconds. We fulfill a client order, take a phone call from our aging mother, send flowers via an online service to a friend, and answer a colleague's question all within a few minutes. All the while our energy dwindles, draining us of precious resources of focus and balance. Leisure time is an oasis in which we suspend all our roles. When you defract your energy in two or more ways, it is as if you are splitting your attention from the very beginning, splaying your thoughts and actions, resulting in less efficiency. Task-switching, as we addressed in chapter 2, wastes a lot of energy as we downshift and upshift, depending on what is happening at the moment.

The rule of full states you expend the least amount of energy by concentrating on one thing at a time. Full means full-on focus, as opposed to half focus on various items that leads to jumbled thinking or worse, paralysis. We addressed the benefits of completing one task before moving on to the next earlier, and we will address the importance of focus later on. For now, it is notable to mention that the rule of full applies to our leisure time, too.

The rule of full does not allow for electronic devices that disturb your free time. Professor Dov Eden and his colleagues have found that *fully* unplugged leisure time for a long weekend is even more restful than a two-week poolside BlackBerrying fest in between dips in the pool. Resist taking a hybrid vacation by fully embracing your downtime.

Follow the rule of full by clarifying ahead of time when you are not available. Do not take client calls on your time off, even if you think it would be okay to sneak in client contact during "dead time." It is not. Avoiding client calls at designated times teaches people what to expect from you. The rule of full is *not* about not going the extra mile. It is about filling up your tank so you can.

Teaching people how to treat you is far more effective than catering to people's every whim at every moment, especially during the hard-earned moments of leisure you need in order to honor your own sanity. As one client told me, saying no to him means I'm actually listening to his request in the first place.

Principle #9: Return to the Classroom

If taking a long weekend seems virtually impossible to you, at least you can give your mind a mini-vacation. A mental holiday can serve to regenerate you in a short period of time. As we have seen, unplugging is a key component to the sustained effects of leisure. Respite relief is also possible if you expose yourself to new ideas, even if you don't leave your usual surroundings.

Adult education is a thriving business with offerings going beyond basket-weaving for boomers. In 2003, the percentage of adults who have obtained a high school or college degree was at an all-time high (85 percent and 27 percent, respectively).[8] According to a U.S. Census Bureau report for 2006, 6.6 percent of the population had attended an adult education class that year. Education is a recognized pathway to economic success later in life, and it comes in many forms. Today you can attend night school, online universities, or non–university affiliated centers to learn more about the world.

In this exercise, research area adult education centers and look for a class that might interest you. Perhaps it is simply an evening lecture on an intriguing topic or a series of classes in which you learn a new skill. Distance learning courses are also available for people with less mobility. Whichever course you choose, you will notice how it adds to the quality of your life as you spend your leisure time doing something you love. It actually saves you time in the long run as you enrich your mind, boost your creativity, and refresh your thoughts.

Principle #10: Visit the Great Outdoors

Outdoor recreation is at its lowest popularity in history as people spend more and more time indoors. Children's roaming radius around their own homes is tighter than ever as parents' fear is at an all-time high. Being outside has become a more rare experience, albeit an essential one. Researchers have linked childhood obesity with the distance of nature from living space: the farther away the green space, the higher the tendency for being overweight.

National parks are a vast resource for recreation and fun. In the United States alone, there are 391 national parks in total, with at least one park in every state (except Delaware), as well as in the District of Columbia, American Samoa, Guam, Puerto Rico, and the Virgin Islands. Yet the annual number of visitors has consistently gone down over the past few years. In 2006 more than 272 million people had visited the national park system in the United States. The following year, only about 224 million people had. The downward trend may be due to the rise in oil prices in recent years, increased admission fees, or a general lack of interest as demographics shift to more single households. Traditionally family-based, national parks in some areas have started adapting to the shift in visitors by offering larger picnic tables to accommodate Hispanic vacationers who tend to travel with extended family members.

While amusement parks continue to enjoy healthy numbers of thrill-seekers, the popularity of outdoor activities has shrunk considerably. A daily dose of fresh air seems to be a thing of the past as people flock to indoor recreational offerings. It's time for a change—and a gulp of oxygen.

John Locke, CEO of a small technology consulting firm based in Seattle, cherishes his time outdoors, as it helps him break away from the linear thinking of business. In his twenties he used to engage in extreme sports such as white-water kayaking, thousand-mile bike tours, and the like. When he started his business, the frequency of his outdoor activities was reduced by 90 percent. Nonetheless, he values being outside not only for the obvious benefits of vitamin D and sunlight but also because it nourishes his creativity. "Rest, and the mental breaks that outdoor activities provide, are crucial to the creative process," he told me. "They are perhaps more important than another few hours of focus on a problem. Currently, my creative focus is on my business: shaping it, building it, directing it into something new. Like all other creative pursuits, having that downtime is critical to success."

The next time you plan some time off, consider tackling the great outdoors. Take a hike in the literal sense of the phrase.

Final Word

Leisure comes in many forms. In this chapter we have reviewed various ways to raise your awareness level about how you view leisure time, what you might do with it, and how you can spend it powerfully. We dusted off our flip-flops to measure our speed, redefined our sense of purpose to make room for time off, listed what we love and why we think we might not get it, examined when free time is a benefit or burden, introduced the absence test, inspired open-ended social events, refined the art of hanging out, applied the rule of full, returned to the classroom, and enjoyed the great outdoors. Free time offers a longer opportunity to relax than daily time-outs, yet both are equally significant in shifting your perspective about time. In the next chapter, you will learn ways to take a breather even when extended leisure isn't in the cards.

7

Time-Outs: Ten Ways to Higher Efficiency

EVEN THEY AGREE *THAT* I NEED TO RELAX.

Haste maketh waste.

—John Heywood (1546)

The Japanese concept of *ma* refers to the space between things. Originally used in relation to the arts, *ma* is associated with rhythm, such as the cadence of speech during a theatrical performance. Dramatic pauses, such as those actors use for effect, are described as *ma*. The space between notes is a similar expression of *ma*, the empty holding place that enhances the art form itself. It literally translates to mean "full of nothingness" and is honored just as the silence between a question and its answer is. It is customary in Japan to wait much longer for a response to a posed question than in the United States, where answers are expected relatively immediately. Europeans are also known for thinking things through with more caution before acting than Americans. Americans, on the other hand, tend to value immediate action between thoughts. We have an idea; then we jump into action. The "just do it" principle is great for offsetting procrastination, as we mentioned in chapter 5. It is also great for overcoming barriers in our lives with a go-for-it attitude. *Ma* is the counterbalance to "just do it." It is the space required to bring respite to our lives and to bridle our impulsiveness when doing something without thinking is inappropriate.

We are uncomfortable with silence in conversation, so it is no wonder we are uncomfortable with silence in our lives. It is perhaps why the idea of taking a time-out is so hard for Americans to grasp.

Our compulsion for permanent motion may stem in part from the pioneer spirit our forefathers were imbued with as they explored the New World. The pursuit of freedom and happiness are principles on which our country is based. After all, we can thank our Puritan work ethic for having achieved so much in such a short time. The history of the United States spans roughly the same length of time as the Renaissance in Europe, for instance. Compare the time of a single epoch in Europe to America's entire existence, and you can start to see where our addiction to speed originates. We built our country on sweat equity, adventure, and great ideas. In an environment that cherishes newness, there's no time for play. Life is serious business.

*   *   *

In 2007, there were 153.1 million workers in the United States.[1] In the same year, the average American employee spent 7.6 hours per day at work, 8.4 hours on average for men and 7.2 hours for women. In their leisure time, women spent roughly twice as much time chatting on the phone, dealing with mail, and answering e-mails than men.[2] Watching television and socializing were the top two leisure activities in which both men and women engaged. The estimates for the average amount of sleep per night that an American gets range between 6.85 and 8.43 hours. We're a nation that sleeps as much as we work, but what do we do in between? It seems we engage in too little, fulfilling play.

The trouble is all work and no play make Jack and Jane just plain dull. In fact, burnout syndrome, a condition of exhausted adrenal glands once reserved for top-ranking executives, can be seen across many industries, including the fields of health care, air traffic transportation, and law enforcement. Mental distress, physical exhaustion, chronic fatigue, insomnia, and heart failure are pervasive throughout the population. One of the primary reasons for these conditions is the fact that we've lost our ability to apply adventure to anything other than work. As we discussed in chapter 6, leisure time is a necessary component for high productivity. Because the areas of work and play have begun to meld in our 24/7 world, we need to consciously take moments to unplug ourselves from the digital rat race. In *Unplugged Play*, Bobbi Conner supports the notion of imaginative, nondigitalized play for kids. Daily gadget-free time-outs for adults are equally important. Putting a little *ma* into our day can make all the difference between efficiency and deficiency. In this chapter we will explore ways to recapture the space between thought and action.

Principle #1: Create a Walking Team

The IT profession is notorious for its long workdays and the endless grind necessary to maintain a company's competitive edge. Australia-based IT worker Andrew Martin devised a way to utilize his lunch hour productively while strengthening the collective spirit in the office. He started a lunchtime walking team. Every day a group of workers walks around the city for thirty-five to forty minutes, downloading their thoughts and feelings about anything from family to the latest project woes. By providing those quiet moments during the workday, Andrew has helped people work through serious issues such as grieving after the loss of a parent, as well as office-related matters. "It really comes down to walking, talking, and dealing with people," Andrew wrote. "It makes a world of difference to my attitude and energy later in the day, too." His boss is less enthused by his rainy-day quiet-time solution of building his model train set at lunch. While his boss views it as nonproductive, it is his lunch hour and he, like the rest of the walking team, knows it sustains his energy level the whole day long.

Besides being great exercise, walking can have other benefits, too. If you live or work near a pedestrian area of any kind, a quick jaunt there can boost your self-esteem considerably. Much like the guilt-free play from chapter 6, a quick twenty-minute time-out from your desk can elevate your mood. Natural light exposure, especially in more northern climes, boosts your immune system as you collect important vitamin D–enriched sunlight.

Whether you work in an office environment or not, gather a group of people for a regular walking tour. Or go it alone through a green space near you. Carl Honoré, author of *In Praise of Slow*, suggests taking a leisurely walk in nature to clear your head. When I asked him how he gets the most enjoyment out of leisure walks, Carl admitted to me that he prefers gadget-free interaction with nature. No MP3 players or iPods are allowed, especially when he goes with his kids. "We meander along gently, open to whatever smells, sounds, or sights nature throws at us. We might stop to climb a fallen log, drop sticks into a stream, or watch a bird building a nest. We chat about this and that or play hide-and-seek. It's all about the journey rather than the destination. And it is always exhilarating."

The power of slow can be unleashed even as you walk briskly, but challenge yourself to go at a slower pace than usual. You might find it difficult at first. Test your pace. If you can still walk and talk without losing your breath, you are at just the right speed.

Principle #2: Protect the American Dream—Take a Nap

To quote Nancy Gibbs, "With too little sleep there are too few dreams."[3] How can you pursue the American Dream if you aren't getting enough shut-eye to let that dream unfold? Sleep and fulfilled dreams go hand in hand.

Sleep deprivation is a debilitating state that can lead to a series of chronic health conditions. Scientists conducted an experiment with volunteers who were kept awake until 3 A.M. for just a few nights. The participants quickly showed a drop in their immune hormones, making them more vulnerable to infections. In another study of healthy young men, University of Chicago's Dr. Eve Van Cauter found that after restricting their night's sleep to four hours for six consecutive nights, their blood sugar levels resembled a pattern associated with weight gain and the early onset of diabetes. The participants' ability to process blood sugar was reduced by 30 percent, their insulin response dropped dramatically, and high levels of the stress hormone cortisol were detected. In short, sleep deprivation is not a good idea.

Images of the overworked, sleep-deprived American are common. But is there truth to them? A recent National Sleep Foundation study that claimed Americans are sleeping less than a generation ago asked participants to *estimate* how much sleep they got each night and came up with an average total of forty-eight hours a week. In 1960, a National Cancer Society survey revealed Americans were getting about eight and a half hours of sleep a night. In a 2008 University of Maryland report, research-ers strictly measured *actual* snooze time, which amounted to an average of fifty-nine hours per week, the same as the National Cancer Society numbers in 1960. The varying results prove the point of the power of slow: people's perceived time is often shorter than the quantified time they actually spend on tasks, including sleep.

In a *Washington Post* article, John P. Robinson, a sociology professor at the University of Maryland who co-authored the study "Not So Deprived: Sleep in America, 1965–2005," is quoted as saying: "It's a status symbol. If you are a good American, you work all hours. It's virtuous in American society to not get enough sleep."[4] Sleep deprivation is somehow a badge of honor, as if we are good citizens for staying up all hours of the night. But as we have already seen in chapter 6, respite is equally important to the overall quality of life in work and in play.

Taking a power nap is a fabulous way to regenerate without entering a full-blown cycle of sleep, which tends to tamper with the body's inner clock. In several studies on airline pilots, a twenty-minute snooze brought the pilots studied back to 100 percent alertness. Whether you are sleep-deprived or not, a little midday siesta can bring you back to morning level concentration within a very short time. Alertness leads to higher productivity and saved time, too.

Large corporations such as Google, Pizza Hut, and Procter & Gamble have seen the benefits of workplace napping. They've even invested in zero-gravity sleeping pods for stressed-out workers to grab some shut-eye before returning to work. Even flight personnel get to lie down. On transatlantic flights it is typically for eighty minutes of rest. On longer flights, they are permitted to sleep in specially made beds for several hours at a time. Airline pilots enjoy the same type of respite on lengthier hauls.

If you are not lucky enough to work at a place that provides your own personal sleeping quarters, you don't need an expensive snooze recliner to catch some sleep during the day. As a health promotion supervisor at the University of California at Davis, Michelle Johnston practices what she preaches about wellness and personal time-outs to the student body. To find herself a moment of solace, Michelle retreats to her car for a nap during her lunch break. She sets her cell phone alarm for twenty minutes while recharging her batteries for the afternoon. Respite can be had in the simplest of places without the techno gizmos available today.

Principle #3: Simply Lift a Finger

A midday nap in a cocoon or car may not be suitable for everyone's situation, but there are ways to simulate sleep even when you can't take a power snooze. Hypnosis is an approach used often for smoking cessation and weight loss that can also be used to rejuvenate yourself. It affects the subconscious mind to give you a deeper sense of control. A side effect is the feeling of time expansion or contraction you get when applying this principle. Even self-hypnosis can serve to reposition your sense of time.

Behavioral psychologist and hypnotherapist Mary Lee La-Bay recommends a simple exercise you can do at your desk, in your parked car, or even in the restroom at work. It is as simple as lifting a finger.

Support your hand on a table or your lap. Relax your body and close your eyes. As you breathe in deeply, say to yourself "one hour." As you say the hour, gently open your eyes and lift your index finger. As you exhale, lower your finger and close your eyes again. Slowly repeat this routine, saying "two hours," "three hours," and on up to "eight hours."

You will begin to notice a change in your alertness as you breathe in and out. While this won't replace actually getting a full night's rest, it will serve to restore you in a pinch. It is a great method for rejuvenating yourself while recovering from jet lag or after a short night's sleep.

Hypnosis, which refers to a heightened wakeful state, brings about a deeper awareness and level of relaxation that your conscious mind cannot achieve on its own. In 1971, Philip Zimbardo and his team of psychologists at Stanford University and the University of California at Berkeley conducted an experiment with a hypnotized group of college students, instructing them to allow the present to expand while allowing both past and future to ebb into the distance without significance. Zimbardo found students were able to distort their perception of time and vastly increase their comprehension of language, setting, thought processes, and social awareness in the present moment. His experiment proved we are capable, much like the Zen masters, to expand our sense of time by altering our awareness.[5]

Principle #4: Take Your Breath Back, Not Away

To borrow a phrase, breathing easier in the harness is a prerequisite for rapid relaxation. As we all know, exercise is a crucial component to anyone's well-being, but we can't always get to the gym as often as we'd like. Learning correct breathing techniques can improve your efficiency and well-being in many ways.

Incorrect breathing not only reduces your productivity levels, it can also lead to an increase in your heart rate, especially at night. In fact, in a November 2007 study conducted by Dr. Matthew T. Naughton of Alfred Hospital and Monash University in Melbourne, Australia, researchers saw a direct link between faulty nighttime breathing and heart failure in patients. Sleep apnea, the most common symptom of which is snoring and daytime sleepiness, literally quickens the pulse as the body struggles to take in oxygen. "Heart rate patterns are influenced enormously by breathing patterns," said Dr. Naughton.[6]

During the day, incorrect breathing can have a similar effect. As stress mounts and stocks tumble, many Wall Street workers hit downtown yoga studios such as Namaste New York to release tension. Yoga, known for its mind-body-spirit connection achieved through breathing and stretching techniques, has become a common form of exercise for overworked executives. According to the magazine *Yoga Journal*, yoga is a $5.7 billion annual industry. It attracts all kinds of people who are looking for a more suitable pace of life.

Professional yoga therapist Felice Rhiannon uses a one-minute breath practice whenever she's feeling frazzled or restless. It is a centering activity based on a slow inhalation and an incremental increase in the length of exhalations.

Inhale to the count of two
Exhale to the count of two
Inhale to the count of two
Exhale to the count of three
Inhale to the count of two
Exhale to the count of four
Inhale to the count of two
Exhale to the count of five

Repeat several times, then return to your normal breathing.

Breath and productivity go hand in hand. Improved breathing regulates the oxygen flow in your blood, making you more alert. With a sharper focus, you can stay on task and make fewer mistakes, thereby saving you time in the long run.

Principle #5: Explore New Places

A change of scenery is a stimulating way to spur your creativity. In *The Artist's Way*, Julie Cameron discusses artist breaks as a way to gather fresh ideas. Browsing your favorite card shop or retreating to a city park for twenty minutes can lead to new ways of thinking. Whether you are struggling with a troubling project or working on your latest novel, creative breaks in stimulating surroundings can give you the gentle nudge you need.

In this exercise, grab a pen and paper and your Yellow Pages. Because this is a multisensory exercise, avoid using the computer to conduct your search. The look, feel, and smell of the paper is important as you literally let your fingers do the walking. Look up a few places in your area you have never been. Note them on your list. Perhaps you've always wanted to find a new flower shop, but have never taken the time to move beyond your immediate neighborhood. Visit the store the next time you are in the area or plan a time to go there. If you are feeling really adventurous, branch out beyond your immediate vicinity to a new part of town. Explore the restaurants and make a lunch reservation with an old friend at the one you like best. Write down any new ideas you may have during or after the experience. As you enjoy your time-out in unfamiliar surroundings, notice how your senses are enlivened by the experience.

Exploring new places shakes up your routine. As creatures of habit, we tend to remain within our comfort zone. Pushing our own self-induced limits unleashes an enormous amount of energy and creativity. It may be as simple as changing your lunchtime routine one day a week. Make Tuesdays your exploration day, for instance. Commit yourself to trying out a new place just to see how it feels. Muster the courage to make mistakes. Tell yourself it is okay to have a bad experience at a restaurant or new shop. Creating the opening to try new things is the point of this exercise. A quick time-out to prove to yourself you are flexible in how you spend your time will also positively impact the flexibility in your thinking.

Principle #6: The Fork Method

We all know we are what we eat. But did you know you are *how* you eat, too? The way in which you spend your mealtimes can greatly influence your well-being. The irony is, the slower you enjoy your meal, the more time you can add to your calendar in the long run.

According to the Eating and Health Module of the American Time Use Survey in 2006, which relies on self-reported activities from a single household within a twenty-four-hour period of time, the average American spends sixty-seven minutes a day eating or drinking as a primary activity. The top three places were at home (67.2 percent), the workplace (12.9 percent), or at an eating establishment (11.2 percent). An additional sixteen minutes of eating and forty-two minutes of drinking as a secondary activity, such as while watching television, playing sports, or working, were reported. In fact, two-thirds of the 29.2 percent of responders who ate while doing something else reported watching television as their primary activity.[7]

In a well-founded group of studies funded by National Food Service Management Institute (NFSMI), the average amount of time it took K–12 students to consume their lunches was between seven and ten minutes. According to nourishment counselor Jeanette Bronée, the average time spent eating a meal in a fast-food restaurant is eleven minutes. In a workplace cafeteria, an average meal is extended by only two more minutes, and a moderately priced restaurant meal lasts a leisurely twenty-eight minutes. All told, we spend little over one hour enjoying our food each day. Speed has entered the dining room, if you happen to eat there at all.

If you belong to the clean-your-plate-*fast* club, consider trying the following exercise the next time you sit down for a meal.

Clock yourself while you eat. Be sure not to engage in any other activity such as reading or watching television. Chances are you will have finished your meal in under a quarter-hour period of time. For your next meal, try this approach: After each bite, place your fork back on the plate. Most of us have gotten used to eating convenience foods that rarely require utensils. For this method, it is best to use a fork with your meal to signal the space between bites. For the duration of your meal, use a fork, and possibly a knife, to eat. By placing your utensils back on the plate after every single bite, you will be forced to slow down automatically. Chew your food thoroughly, then pick the fork back up for the next bite. Chewing is important as it releases essential enzymes to break down the food into digestible bites. The better you chew, the better your system can process the food you've ingested. Using this fork method, you will extend your meal by several minutes. Clock yourself again to see how much you have slowed down.

As a rule, it is best not to read or watch television while you eat. As we have seen in chapter 2, disregarding your internal cues by distracting yourself with other things often leads to overeating.

A USDA report on nutritional knowledge as a basis for food choice found that time pressure overrode a person's prior understanding of healthy meals.[8] In other words, if people are hungry or stressed, they will eat what is most readily available to them, even if it is not the healthiest choice. It is another example of how slowing down can tip your life balance in your favor.

You may ask yourself what eating slowly has to do with saving time. It actually takes the brain twenty minutes to recognize it is full. By eating mindfully, you are more likely to eat less than if you were to gobble your food quickly. Eating slowly aids in the digestion process, making you less sluggish and leading to a decreased need to grab yet another cup of coffee in the afternoon. Changing your eating habits even slightly will result in overall improvement in your well-being, which will ultimately save you time and, possibly, heartburn, too.

Principle #7: Where's the *Ma*?

At the beginning of this chapter, we discussed the Japanese term *ma*, or the space between things. If you were to look at your calendar, would you see any wiggle room between events or would you find you have a seamless list of to-dos every day? Do you allow for downtime between meetings or appointments or do you live with a constant sense of immediacy? The importance of downtime can be seen by watching children whose naptime schedule is as precious to their parents as their own timetables. If you have ever witnessed a toddler in need of a nap, you will know how important *ma* truly is for human beings. We know napping is good for anyone. In this exercise, we will make another case for a little more *ma* in our lives, too.

Efficiency implies you are not running around putting out one fire after the other. It suggests you have a plan that you can execute with the help of identifiable milestones. When you create breathing room between the milestones, you are more easily able to sustain your energy throughout the entire day. This does not mean you indulge in procrastination, but rather in purposeful rest to maintain your balance. If you live in the country, you know how a visit to a major city feels hectic, invigorating, and stressful. Some people thrive on the fast-paced lifestyle, but city dwellers and country folk alike need moments of solace to process their day. In a Chicago suburb, one educational content company that contributes to K–12 textbooks has devised a way to bring *ma* to the workday itself.

The CEO and president of Shakespeare Squared, Kim Kleeman, designed a stress management room to alleviate the tension created by her company's deadline-driven environment. Complete with soothing music and dim lighting, the room is a *ma*-dedicated space for her employees to recharge their batteries after staring at their monitors all day. The room is off-limits to more than one person at a time, except during the company's monthly massages.

In this exercise, find a *ma* moment in your day when you can close your eyes without sleeping. Shut out the din of your daily environment using earplugs or a quiet room off the beaten path. Use an eye mask or kerchief to shut out any light if you have no window shades. In between appointments, close out the world for a few minutes to center yourself. Honor your *ma* as you would your own mother. A *ma* moment can often lead to an epiphany as you release the tension and make way for higher creativity.

Ma can save you time as the space holder between thought and action. Before you jump into the very next thing, take a step back and look at the big picture. Harness your impulsiveness by refraining from jumping into something that might not serve you long-term. Carving out a *ma* moment can help you see the impact of your ideas more clearly.

Principle #8: Aromatherapy

We all have days when we feel we cannot breathe due to our crushing schedules. When all else fails, you can add a dash of scent to your day without adding to the pressure. Your olfactory cells can be a potent tool in your quest for a daily time-out. Aromatherapy is a proven method for promoting relaxation or alertness. Depending on your mood on any given day, use the following chart to help you select the most appropriate essential oil. In choosing the right oil line for the greatest effect, be sure you get essential oils that are pure and not mixed with fillers. There has been evidence that synthetic fillers are actually harmful. Check the label for words such as "organic," "natural," or "wild-crafted," as they contain the highest purity of oil. Some are extracted through a heating process called steam distillation. This process is used for leaves, bark, and petals, for instance. Cold-pressed extraction is used in particular for citrus peels such as orange or tangerine.

According to classical homeopath Krista J. Essler, alcohol extraction is also an acceptable method without toxicity. "Other solvents, such as hexane or petroleum benzene," she warns, "are toxic and cannot be totally separated from the oils after the extraction process is complete." It is advisable to stick with the organic offerings in your local health food store to ensure the best quality. Consult an expert to help you with your selection if you are uncertain.

Utilize the power of smell by purchasing an aromatherapy lamp and some tea lights. Add up to five drops of aromatherapy oil to the lamp's water-filled basin. Place the candle underneath the basin, then light it. Be sure you have enough water in the lamp, as it tends to evaporate rather quickly. Keep the flame away from any papers on your desk, but be sure the lamp is close enough to you so you can smell its subtle aroma. If you work in an office environment that doesn't allow an open flame, place several dabs of oil on a tissue and put it up to your nose periodically. Women can tuck a scented tissue or handkerchief inside their shirts for continuous contact with the oil.

Basic essential oils organized by mood:	
Agitation	frankincense, geranium, lavender, rosewood, ylang-ylang
Anger	frankincense, lavender, lemon, orange, ylang-ylang
Anxiety	orange, ylang-ylang
Depression	frankincense, geranium, grapefruit, lavender, lemon, ylang-ylang

Disappointment	frankincense, geranium, lavender, orange, spruce, ylang-ylang
Discouragement	frankincense, geranium, lavender, lemon, orange, Roman chamomile, rosewood, spruce
Distraction	lavender, lemon, orange, peppermint, ylang-ylang
Fear	geranium, orange, spruce, ylang-ylang
Frustration	frankincense, lavender, lemon, orange, peppermint, spruce, ylang-ylang
Grief	Roman chamomile, lavender
Guilt	frankincense, geranium, lemon, spruce
Insomnia	frankincense, lavender
Irritability	geranium, lavender, lemon, peppermint, spruce, ylang-ylang
Obsession	geranium, lavender, ylang-ylang

Many thanks to Krista J. Essler for helping me compile this list.

Principle #9: Sound Therapy

Much like aromatherapy, therapy with sound has a proven effect on relaxing your body for a quick time-out during the day. Although it is a relatively new field, it has already started making headway around the world. According to the British Academy of Sound Therapy, our bodies are made up of sound waves that consistently move. After particularly stressful moments, our energy tips off balance. Sound therapists utilize sonic frequencies such as music or the sounds of nature to interact with our own sound waves, thus realigning our corporeal energy waves to their original balanced state. One CEO of a boutique public relations firm in Charlottesville, Virginia, swears by her dolphins CD that mimics ocean waves and dolphin song. After particularly stressful days, she pops it into her CD player as a sleeping aid.

According to a report presented at the American Heart Association's 62nd Annual Fall Conference of the Council for High Blood Pressure Research, a twelve-minute binaural (both ears) audio therapy program with ocean waves and a calming voiceover lowered blood pressure even more in all twenty of the patients than the group of twenty-one that listened to a Mozart sonata of equal length. The lead author of the study and assistant professor in the College of Nursing at Seattle University, Jean Tang, is quoted in *Therapy Times* as saying "The binaural sound regulates the brain waves to the alpha range, which produces a calming effect allowing participants to concentrate. The relaxation method affects the parasympathetic nervous system, which lowers the blood pressure by relaxing the blood vessels."[9]

When part-time musician David Schwartz plays his Native American flutes, he himself is entranced by the sounds the instruments make. When he plays for larger audiences, he inevitably gets approached by people afterward who have had a transcendent experience during his performance. "The only aspect of time that I experience is the transitions between notes, and that's just more of a sequential rhythm," he wrote to me in an e-mail. "I have no idea how long I play, although when I time my songs, they tend to run from two to four minutes." He has done freestyle playing with other musicians that has gone on for twenty or thirty minutes, although he was completely unaware of the time that had passed. Music can put you in a trancelike state, making time completely irrelevant to the experience itself.

Therapeutic sound can be made in many ways. Himalayan singing bowls, metal bowls that are struck with mallets so that they "sing," have been used for centuries during Buddhist meditation, prayer, and trance induction. In some countries, such as Japan and Vietnam, the bowls are used to signal the passage of time or a change of events. They are, if you will, a type of clock marking time and transition.

Whatever sound you choose to induce a moment of relaxation in your day, make sure it is easily accessible when you need it. Whether in your iPod, car stereo, or CD player at home, flip on a moment of calming sound to tune out the noise in your life. It could be incessant office chatter, a neighbor's screaming infant, or commuter traffic that unnerves you. Replace the din with an uplifting sonic environment to ease the tension.

Principle #10: Color Therapy*

As with smells and sounds, your sight impacts your mood, too. The well-researched area of color therapy in the health-care and wellness industries tells us which colors to avoid and

---

*This color analysis is also used to explain the various chakras in energy and healing work, which we will not discuss here.

which to embrace for our overall sense of well-being. Advertisers rely on color schemes to create emotions in their prospective customers. Have you ever wondered why price tags indicating a price reduction are typically red or orange? These bright colors demand attention, creating a sense of urgency in the buyer. They might as well shout at you, and you often jump into action as a result. As we all know, red is the color of appetite and passion, while green reflects serenity, calm, and coolness.

Color	Positives	Negatives	Therapeutic Quality
Red	courage, pioneering spirit, leadership, strong will, confidence, determination, high energy, spontaneity	fear of progress, general fearfulness, ruthlessness, aggression, dominance, resentment, self-pity, stubbornness, quick-temperedness	energizing, stimulates appetite, revitalizing
Orange	joy, enthusiasm, independence, sociability, constructiveness, creativity	exhibitionism, despondency, difficulty interacting with others, pride	energizing, stimulating, warming, excellent for creativity
Yellow	open-mindedness, wisdom, confidence, logic, humor, intellect	vanity, vindictiveness, pessimism, cowardice	warming, stimulating, helps with concentration

Color	Positives	Negatives	Therapeutic Quality
Green	generosity, compassion, sympathy, understanding, harmony, adaptability	unscrupulousness with money, indifference, jealousy, stinginess, lack of consideration	rebalancing, especially after trauma, harmonious
Blue	Loyalty, tact, trustworthiness, peacefulness	self-righteousness, coldness, lack of trustworthiness	calming, relaxing, healing
Indigo	intuition, faithfulness, unity, articulateness	separation, fearfulness, lack of tolerance, tendency to be judgmental	quieting, contemplative, sedative
Violet	reverence, advanced mental powers, kindness, justice	feelings of superiority, flaunting of power, lack of other-oriented behavior	spiritual, meditative

Source: Adapted with permission from Colourtherapyhealing.com

While there are limitless shades of color, this simplified chart tells you which colors evoke which emotions and character traits in people.

How does color save you time? The better you feel in your environment, the more productive you are. An artist's palette can whet your palate and your appetite for life, too. As you embrace your surroundings, you become more intimate with your own personal bank account of time.

Final Word

We have seen how quick time-outs can lead to higher productivity throughout the day. A moment of solace enjoyed through a walking group, some organized shut-eye, self-hypnosis, powerful breath, exploration, and chewing slowly remind us about the power of slow. Honoring the space between things and acknowledging the instrumentality of smell, sound, and color give way to a more mindful pace of life. We can adjust our routines and environments to be more in alignment with who we are so we can be the best we can be. Celebrate your new milestone in pursuing the slow life. Ask others to join you. We do not live in a vacuum, but in fellowship with others. Now it's time to get the people in your life on board by managing their expectations so they can live the power of slow, too.

Expectation Management:
Ten Ways to Tame the Gimme Gremlin

Whatever we expect with confidence becomes our own self-fulfilling prophecy.

—Brian Tracy

Managing expectations may seem like a time-robbing activity, but the reality is expectations are a part of life. Automobile traffic would not work effectively if people didn't expect everyone to follow the rules of the road. We expect to receive the correct change at the store, to get honest feedback from our closest friends, and to hear a dial tone when we pick up the phone to call someone. We are all about expectations. By managing them well, we teach others how to treat us, too.

When you manage expectations, you are showing others what the future holds for them. Effective expectation management will save you more time and grief than you could possibly imagine. You build loyalty and trust in other people as you show them what to expect from you. While it may be hard to identify people's expectations, or even your own, it is best to assume that people always have a certain level of expectation about things. The trick is finding out what those expectations are so you can manage them to the best of your ability.

Let's take a real-life example. When the wind blows your clothes off the line, do you get mad? The wind is simply doing what it does best. It blows. Perhaps it isn't the wind that makes you angry, but the unfulfilled expectation that your clothes should stay clean and dry on the line. You think you are safe in your assumption that they will remain where you put them. But change happens, often unexpectedly.

Thwarted intentions and unfulfilled expectations are the leading cause of upset. If we don't get what we want, we are dismayed, sometimes even infuriated. We spend a lot of our time throwing an adult-size tantrum about our unfulfilled vision. The trouble is we often don't even realize we have an expectation of the way things should be. Consequently, we can't identify the source of our upset. We only know that we are disappointed.

Drawing on the discipline of project management, we can apply the powerful principles of expectation management to our work and personal lives. According to an IBM-based theory called four quadrant expectation management, managing expectations can be defined as "a formal process to continuously capture, document, and maintain the content, dependencies, and sureness of the expectations for persons participating in an interaction, and to apply the information to make the interaction successful."[1] In other words, you communicate internal, external, perceived, and stated expectations with the intention of fulfilling them. The fuel to run your expectation management engine is communication. Unfulfilled or poorly managed expectations are some of the biggest time vampires ever. The Gimme Gremlin emerges as you fall in a downward spiral of miscommunication and frustration.

The Gimme Gremlins are the kinds of people who are never satisfied. They set unrealistic expectations for themselves and others. They leave upset in their wake and if you're not careful, you might get swept up in the wave, too. They have not learned how to self-adjust, to check in with themselves and others, and to communicate their intentions.

In this chapter, we will examine ways in which you can successfully manage expectations to engage in a more powerful relationship with others and with time itself. We are going to slay the Gimme Gremlin, so get ready. It's easier than you think.

Principle #1: Identifying Expectations

According to high-performance coach and sales trainer John Nelson, people do not argue with their own data. In other words, they will not readily put their own beliefs into question. This is the reason why it is important to find out what people's expectations are in the beginning before managing them is even possible. He identifies two sets of expectations we need to be aware of when communicating with others: conscious and subconscious expectations. For conscious expectations to be teased out, you need to do two things: ask questions (discovery phase) and make agreements (contract phase). For instance, ask people what they want and why they want it. Have them tell you about a time they did not receive what they wanted. At this point, you will start to learn whether you can work with the person or not. As John notes, oftentimes your own expectations will begin to shift during the discovery process. The result is an agreement based on a mutual understanding you developed during the exploration process.

Once you have identified a person's conscious expectations, you can begin to move to the subconscious ones. They are best handled by building rapport with the person. While only 7 percent of *what* is said gets translated by the other person, *how* it is said, through tone, body language, and volume, has the most lasting impact. As the famous saying goes, people may not remember what you say, but they will always remember how you make them feel.

A longtime school principal, Werner Manke recollects how his leadership style changed when he realized commitment to a solid vision coupled with hard work was not enough to get the job done. What he terms his "bulldozer style of leadership" often left people cold. He soon realized he would have to turn into a gentle gardener, nurturing relationships and often just listening to others to learn of their expectations and gain their respect. "I found by concentrating on building relationships rather than trying to mold and shape people into my own ideal, I realized more success." One cold winter day he opened a locked door for a teacher loaded down with books. As he helped her carry them to her classroom, she mentioned how great it would be to have the doors unlocked and the rooms heated before school started to set the tone for the day. It was an easy task he happily did for her. Her gratitude seeped through the teacher's lounge, and he realized that one gesture had made all the difference. In fulfilling her simple request, Werner set off a ripple effect. He successfully managed his relationships with the entire teaching staff by identifying one teacher's expectation. His willingness to openly communicate and listen to her need had a lasting impact.

This principle involves asking simple questions of people and listening to their answers. Remember, oftentimes it is what is *done*, not said, that carries the most gravity.

Principle #2: Underpromise and Overdeliver

When Andy Abramson was a teen, he served as executive director of Hockey Central, an organization funded by the Philadelphia Flyers in the 1970s and '80s. There he learned a valuable lesson about keeping your word. Several times he encountered some retired athletes who would agree to show up at events, but when it came time to do so, they didn't make the appearance. Someone told Andy that they were simply trying to "be nice." At the ripe age of eighteen, Andy learned it is better to underpromise and overdeliver. It was a lesson he still applies in his business as the CEO of a marketing communications agency today. Trying to be everyone's friend and then not delivering on those promises creates the exact opposite to that which you intended. You end up with a lot of disappointed people in your circle.

People appreciate candor in their relationships. When you only give people partial information, it leads to confusion or, worse, a broken promise. We discussed the importance of keeping your word and how to say no kindly in chapter 4. Setting manageable, attainable, worthwhile expectations makes people feel they've gotten their value from the promise you've made them.

People are often not conscious of the expectations someone else has made for them, yet they exist nonetheless. In business, in particular, it is important not to overpromise what you cannot possibly deliver. As we have learned, saying no to some things does not mean you are saying no to *everything*. A favored line in business is "Here's what I can promise you . . ." It builds trust when you are honest about what the person can expect.

Think about the popularity of the *What to Expect* book series. Everyone likes to have a semblance of control, as if they can know what will happen next, even if life doesn't offer any guarantees. Having milestones to celebrate progress limits uncertainty, a condition most humans wish to avoid.

The secret formula to Starbucks's success, for instance, does not lie in its roasted ground coffee. It lies in the template of expectations its founders laid out from the very beginning. No matter where you are in the world, you know what to expect when you walk into a Starbucks. The logo is the same, the selections are predictable, and even the baked goods resemble what you get at home. You know what you will experience every time you go to one, from Munich to Miami.

For McDonald's as well, success lies in its predictability and branding. From Singapore to Seattle, the kitchen layout is exactly the same. Reproducibility and a shared global experience have made it one of the world's largest corporations. Consumer expectations are fulfilled. Modifications, such as an aberrant interior design or vastly different food selection, would lead to a suboptimal experience. Consistency has taught people what to expect, and it's at the root of their overwhelming success.

Where have you overpromised and underdelivered in your life? Write down ways you can set people's expectations so you keep your word while pleasantly surprising them, too.

Principle #3: Negotiate Face Time

From an employment perspective, managing expectations is essential when designing a work arrangement that helps you function to the best of your ability. Our ability to handle vast amounts of data, for instance, has increased dramatically due to technological advances. In the age of Google, we aren't even required to retain the information, but rather to know where to retrieve it when we need it. As a result, a massive shift in the workplace has occurred. People's work environments have been forever altered with the ability to telecommute some, if not all, of the workweek.

According to WorldatWork, an estimated 45 million Americans telecommuted in 2006, up from 41 million in 2003. As employers react to soaring energy prices, the four-day workweek has been introduced for many workers across the country, including Utah's state employees and custodial staff at

Ohio's Kent State University. Eligible federal government employees are offered four-day workweeks and telecommuting options as well. The face of the workplace is changing. As a result, face time has taken on a newly defined role.

Studies point to the many benefits of telecommuting, including a more organic pace of life to meet the demands of family and work collectively. The lack of face time, however, has been highlighted as the number one challenge for telecommuters, who often appear only sporadically at headquarters. Face time, or the time in which you are present at the office, still holds value for coworkers—for one thing, they do not see their telecommuting colleagues tangibly producing evidence of their work.

Because face time is still an important aspect at many workplaces, negotiating face time is yet another way to manage the expectations of others. Stacy DeBroff, a former attorney who used to run the public interest office at Harvard Law School part time while raising two toddlers, claims "strategic visibility" is a top way to maintain a presence while balancing the demands of life itself. She coins it her Wizard of Oz technique, in which she manages people's high expectations without going under in the process.

"Like the Wizard, I did not want anyone to look behind the kingdom of the public interest office just to find one dashing, slightly frazzled mom behind the curtain," she wrote to me. Instead of being all things to all people, she focused on strategic visibility by scheduling meetings and large events well in advance to match her schedule. She utilized technology such as e-mail updates and frequent newsletters to project a larger image. In addition, she tapped into the power of delegation by bulking up part-time staff hours to field student requests. "Put all together, the students and my boss perceived me as always available and visibly doing a great job. The Wizard of Oz technique enabled me to manage their high expectations of the sun never setting on the public interest kingdom, while a Friday might find me swinging with my kids in a playground or reading books cuddled up on the couch."

For this principle, consider how often you spend time at the office or at a task simply because you think your "face" is required to be there. Whether it's a volunteer position or the workplace environment, you can most likely negotiate less face time and still get the job done by practicing strategic visibility. It's about managing the expectations you have for yourself and those of others, too.

Principle #4: Expectations Are a Two-Way Street

Not only do you need to manage other people's expectations, but it is crucial that you also learn to manage your own. If you are a member of the chronically high expectation club, chances are you spend a great deal of your day unhinged by other people. You would benefit from lowering your expectations to a more manageable height. Let life be your greatest teacher. If your best friend always shows up late, he is teaching you what to expect. You may not be able to change your friend's behavior, but you can change your expectation to match what he is truly capable of.

It is unfair to assume people cannot change, but while they are in the process of realizing what's important to you in order for the relationship to work, lowering your expectations is an important component in avoiding upset and time-wasting misery. At the same time, cutting people some slack doesn't mean they can be slackers; effectively communicating that it is important for you that they be on time will heighten their awareness. Sometimes, raising people's consciousness means you have to take drastic measures.

Former accountant turned speaker Rich DiGirolamo made an appointment one day to meet a friend who was going to deliver some important tax documents to Rich. His chronically late friend was to meet Rich at 2:30 P.M. When his friend did not show a minute later, he stepped back into his car and drove away without the papers in hand. His friend called him on his cell phone around 2:35 P.M., asking him where he was.

"You are always late, and I am no longer waiting for you," Rich responded. It was a liberating moment in which Rich recognized the importance of his time over pleasing others.

"From that day forward I made the decision," Rich wrote me in an e-mail exchange. "I will always start my meetings on time, end on time, and show up places on time. And I will expect this from the other party. If not, I will go about my business. And if the late party has a problem with this, it is now their problem."

Rich's story illustrates a key point in our relationship with time: If we allow others to continuously dishonor our time and theirs, we can never fully come into alignment with time itself. He taught his friend a huge lesson in expectation management. If you expect me to be on time, then I expect the same from you.

Managing your own expectations requires a periodic checking in with your own emotions. Set three intervals throughout the day in which you ask yourself how you are doing. For instance, at the beginning of the day, you can determine what you'd like to accomplish in that day. Perhaps it is painting the garage door, sweeping the porch, and collecting the last few leaves in your yard. By midday, ask yourself again how you are doing. Have you gotten distracted or are you on task? What's your plan of action when you get to four o'clock? What will you do if you don't reach your objectives? What will you do if you do? By the end of the day, you can assess how you did.

This exercise teaches you how to self-adjust and match your expectations with reality.

Principle #5: Leadership Through Expectation Suspension

We all carry some leadership position in our lives: whether it's for the community, our families, or even for ourselves. We are all the masters of our own ship, as we learned in chapter 5. Great leadership requires a strong ability to motivate others and to manage their expectations thoughtfully while fulfilling higher intentions.

Placing expectations on others can lead to a power struggle if you're not careful. According to certified life coach Natalie Tucker Miller, what people truly would like when they have expectations is power. If you wield your power like you would a ninja sword, you'll leave the room empty-handed. Using skilled communication, you can instill in people a sense of confidence and empowerment without creating a winner-take-all scenario.

How do you go about creating a win-win situation? First, you have to clarify what your broader vision is before you can get anyone to work toward that goal. Identify what your vision is by being very specific in your declaration. How many widgets do you want to sell this year? How many friends do you want to make? How often do you want to run a marathon?

Once you have honed the vision, you can tell others. Effectively communicating that vision helps people's understanding of what you expect from them. If this is done well, they will gain ownership of the vision long before it has become reality, raising their own expectations of themselves. A clear vision and clearly communicated expectations go hand in hand.

For instance, let's say you would like to erect a monument in the town square for a famous musician who has brought notoriety to the community. You wouldn't get far in realizing your dream if you didn't enroll others in your vision. And you can only do that if you can clearly state why you think a monument is important, who will benefit, and what the impact will be on the community at large.

As we have mentioned throughout this book, acknowledging people by fully listening to them fosters positive communication. The key step in doing so is to suspend your own expectation: of what you expect them to say, of what you think they are saying, and of what you might say back. Fully listening engages the person in such a way as to disengage from expectations altogether. As you, the listener, lift your expectation, you create a free-flowing atmosphere for your partner to express himself without hindrance. Once the person is finished speaking, it is important to feed back to the person what you heard him say.

Both honoring and enrolling another in your higher purpose is
the sign of true leadership.

Principle #6: Turning the Tables

Growing into leadership can be a daunting experience for
someone who has always been good at what she does, but has
never been accountable to others in a managerial position. As
talented people move up the ranks over the course of their
lives, they are often put in charge of managing other people
which, inevitably, involves managing their expectations, too.

Emmy Award–winning journalist Kare Anderson developed
a surefire way of dealing with other people in the corporate
division she led. She would immediately share her top goal
with the people she had to manage. Each time a new person
was brought into the division or assigned a new task, she
would tell them her top goal for the person, in that job or for
that task. Then, she would ask them to spend some time before meeting again to consider if they had a better goal for
their job or assigned task in light of the top goal of the division, what they needed to succeed, their benchmarks, timetables, and so forth. Also, she asked them how she could best
support them in achieving their top goal. They gained an overall sense of ownership about the task at hand, making it their
responsibility, not hers. They held themselves accountable for
achieving the goal they mutually agreed upon. Further, she
discovered they often set a higher goal and shorter timetable
than she would have set for them. From her work as a *Wall
Street Journal* reporter, she understood that people are more
likely to work harder to prove themselves right than to prove

their boss right. Kare made those who worked for her think for themselves in a side-by-side, not top-down, approach. By partnering with them to ensure their success, she ensured her own. She managed their expectations beautifully by having them be the creators of their own design.

You don't have to be the boss to manage expectations well. Whenever Kathy Slattengren's workaholic boss would ask her to stay late or work weekends at the Seattle-based software development company where she spent twenty years, she would consider the time spent at work as time spent away from her family. As a full-time working mother, she knew she had to balance out her expectations across the board. Most often, she responded by setting his expectations to a standard more in alignment with her comfort level. If it was crunch time or the company had to release software over the weekend, she was happy to do her part. Otherwise, she declined to work later just to please her boss. Given his workaholic tendencies, she knew she could never put in enough time to satisfy him. It didn't impact her ability to obtain a raise or advancement. In fact, she set a new standard for her coworkers, too, who admired her ability to manage their boss's expectations so well. Kathy also encouraged her boss to go home at a reasonable time, especially since he reported his wife was complaining she never got to see him. She successfully turned the tables to a saner, slower pace of life in which enrichment could be had both inside and outside the office.

For this principle, think of ways you can turn the tables to partner with the people around you. How can you create a win-win in which everyone walks away empowered with realistic goals for themselves and others?

Principle #7: Speak the Same Language

If you've ever traveled to a foreign place, you know how disorienting a new environment can be. Everything seems strange—the food, the language, the smells, sights, sounds, you name it. If you don't know the language, you might be able to get by with a few gestures, but you won't be able to have an intelligent conversation about what matters to you most. Consequently, your relationships to others and your surroundings are limited at best. We all know the saying knowledge equals power. Language is the most powerful knowledge of all. Knowing how to speak to people can make the difference between time wasted and a life spent well.

Speaking the same language can help you match your need with your ability to fulfill it. The very same principle applies when managing expectations.

Let's take an example of a husband and wife who have agreed to communicate every day via e-mail during the wife's trip to Europe.

"Give me a report every day about your happenings," the husband says. The wife agrees, tearfully waving good-bye at the airport. She dutifully checks in with him, sends several e-mails, and awaits his reply. He sends none. After calling the neighbor, text-messaging his cell phone, and attempting to instant message him on the home computer, she calls him in hysterics from a pay phone. He picks up on the first ring.

"Why haven't you responded?" she screeches into the mouthpiece.

"You didn't tell me I should."

This example illustrates a classic mismanagement of expectations. The wife promises to write, expecting a response each time she does. The husband merely asks her to write so he knows she's alive and well. The two did not successfully communicate what they expected from each other. In fact, they did not speak the same language at all.

A great way to avoid miscommunication is to use the exact words your partner does. It's called the feedback method of communication. Using the same example from above, the wife could have fed back to her husband what he expected. "You would like me to give you a report every day about my happenings." After repeating what he said almost verbatim, then, in turn, she could have added her request. "And I would love a report from you every day, too, dear." To confirm that he heard her, he would then repeat what she said to him. "And I will send you a report every day, too."

Toronto-based project manager Max Entin practices using the same language to be sure his clients' expectations match what he can deliver. His advice is to repeat periodically the expectations you set out at the beginning so everyone remains on the same page. "In many cases, when setting expectations, people think they understand each other, but in the end it turns out they don't." Using the feedback method to effectively manage people's reality can save you a lot of time in the end. The same-language principle gives people confirmation you have heard them. By feeding back to them what you have said, you reinforce your understanding while acknowledging others *and* their expectations.

Principle #8: Identifying Risk Factors

One underlying principle of expectation management is gaining a clear perspective on the risks involved in an endeavor. In a country of unlimited possibilities, it can be challenging to convince people there are both limitations and risks associated with what you are trying to achieve. The range of available options becomes a double-edged sword: Thinking in terms of possibility liberates you from the shackles of limitations, but not *all* the things you can imagine are desirable. Seeking out possibilities and choosing the one that suits you best are key factors in managing your own expectations and those of others. In this section you will learn to get real about what is possible and what is not by identifying people's tolerance for risk.

Before you embark on a project, sit down with those involved to brainstorm about possibilities. The point is to be realistic about the goals you can achieve in the time allotted. According to *Merriam-Webster's Collegiate Dictionary*, "brainstorming" is defined as "the mulling over of ideas by one or more individuals in an attempt to devise or find a solution to a problem." You must have an exchange of ideas in order to come up with the most suitable method, all the while understanding there are not only rewards, but risks, too. After you have come up with various approaches, define the pros (rewards) and cons (risks) of each possibility. Then rate yourselves by your risk tolerance. It helps tremendously in bringing everyone onto the same page and unearthing any hidden agendas people may have brought into the conversation. Once you have identified the risks, your tolerance for taking chances, and the goals you wish to achieve, you have taken the necessary steps to manage people's expectations successfully.

Public relations professional Paula Lovell approaches her clients with a simple process to align their expectations with reality. She counsels her clients by letting them know her media activity can go one of three ways: the media will report a positive story, a blistering one, or a neutral one with positives and negatives. Before doing anything, she asks her clients a simple question: "What's your appetite for risk?" By doing so, she lets them know the possibilities of what could happen. She calls it her risk-reward analysis, and it successfully manages their expectations every time.

If you want to gauge someone's expectations before conducting business on their behalf, ask them the risk question. It will help them understand what they are getting into. At least they will be informed before asking you to take a leap of faith. The time saved by conducting your due diligence before the fact is immeasurable.

Principle #9: Learning from Failure

No matter how hard we try, there will be moments when we mismanage people's expectations. As I have already mentioned, life is our greatest teacher. When things go awry, ask yourself, "What have I learned from this?" We often learn more from our mistakes than we do from our accomplishments.

When her daughter was eighteen months old, Malaika Rogers, personal assistant to a board member for various financial institutions, had to complete a time-intensive, deadline-driven project for her boss in record time. Known for her organizational ability, Malaika believed she might even finish the project early—that is, until her daughter came down with a fever of 103 degrees Fahrenheit and croup in the middle of the night. She suddenly found herself working only thirty minutes over the following two days when she had planned to spend six hours per day on the project. By day four, Malaika herself came down with the same temperature. Behind schedule, she feverishly plowed through the next week. At one point, she delicately approached her boss with her dilemma of possibly missing deadline. While he was sympathetic to her circumstances, he could not alter the date because the project had already been added to the agenda of the state agency that only met quarterly. A delay would have meant deferred tax credits for an entire year. "My boss views me as a bit of a magician, because I am always able to solve whatever crisis he throws my way in an efficient, timely manner," Malaika wrote. "He figured that this time would be no different, even if the odds were stacked against me." Miraculously, Malaika pulled through despite her severe illness. In the end, she was disappointed in herself. She felt like a failure even though she had met her boss's expectations, because she had failed to meet her own.

Malaika's story is a classic case of mismanaged expectations over time. Her wizardry had served her well in the past, but it came back to haunt her when she met her limitations head-on. Unused to her saying no, Malaika's boss counted on her to come through as she always had. It taught her a valuable lesson in managing people's expectations to allow for human error. Sometimes, our greatest failures are our greatest lessons, too.

In the movie 27 Dresses, Katherine Heigl's character, Jane, is the go-to girl for everyone. Ever the willing one, she manages to be a bridesmaid in twenty-seven weddings before realizing she deserves to get help in her life, too. In a classic bridal shop scene, she confronts her self-centered sister by telling her she is not going to take it anymore. Up to this point in the movie, she had always put a smile on her face and agreed to everything. People simply expected Jane to be accommodating, and she was. She had taught others how to treat her by not managing their expectations at all. It wasn't until she grew a spine that her life, and her love, truly unfolded.

In this exercise, consider where you have mismanaged expectations. Whether they are yours or someone else's, ask yourself what you have learned from it. List steps to conquer the time-sucking activities of pleasing others at the expense of yourself. Remember the phrases from chapter 4. Sometimes expectations can be realigned with a single word—no.

Principle #10: The Meaning of "Now"

The importance of semantics in human communication is underrated. Anyone who has been to New York City and Los Angeles will tell you the simple word "now" has entirely different meanings. "Now" in New York means at the very second you are pointing your finger to the floor with a stern look on your face. "Now" in Los Angeles could mean anywhere from in a few minutes to perhaps never. You can expect when a producer in Los Angeles says he'll call you "right back" that he might not. You just have to keep trying until you hit the perfect moment.

Similarly, any mother will tell you "in a minute" doesn't really mean sixty seconds later. It's the typical response to a nagging child asking to play video games for the seventeenth time. What we say and what we mean are often entirely different things.

Educational consultant Steven Roy Goodman notes that parent-speak is not teen-speak, for instance. When a parent says to get the college application in "by next week," that does not mean "in a week" for many children. It is simply a ballpark time frame they may or may not keep to.

"When my students say they are 'now working on their college essays,'" Steven told me, "their parents hear 'my child is procrastinating again.'" "Now" has a very different meaning for teenagers than it does for their parents. It's the New York–Los Angeles tension all over again. And it leads to mismanaged expectations, arguments, and time-wasting stress.

Cultural understanding is extremely vital for learning what to expect. A Parisian meal might last three hours while an American one might only take fifteen minutes. A Brazilian meeting may not take place at the appointed hour because punctuality in Brazil is not valued as it is elsewhere, and depending on the person's social ranking, he may be delayed by hours. "Now" does not mean "this second" for everyone. A teenager saying she will do it now might actually mean after she does something else.

In this exercise, ask yourself what you mean when you say the word "now." Does it mean within sixty seconds or in twenty minutes after you have completed other tasks? How often do you react right away when someone else says "now"? Do the people in your life share your definition or does it have an entirely different meaning for them? Ask them what "now" means to them. It warrants having a conversation with those people whose definition differs from your own. It helps you learn what to expect from others as you learn more about yourself.

Final Word

Expectations are like the molecules of air we breathe. We don't see them, but we know they are there. Mismanaged expectations take us down Upset Avenue, which leads to stress, wasted time, and a lower quality of life.

In this chapter we explored how to identify expectations, deliver without disappointing, develop a strategic presence, teach people how to treat us, suspend expectations, turn the tables to instill ownership in others, remain on the same page using a common language, determine our risk tolerance, learn from failure, and clarify semantics. Clear, concise communication can give you back the time you might have spent cleaning up whatever problems were created by your lack of clarity in the first place. Your minutes saved are now turning into hours. You're salvaging your personal bank account. The Gimme Gremlin has left the building. What comes next is the importance of focus. It requires commitment, but as you have already proven, you certainly have what it takes.

9

Focus Factor: Ten Ways to Gain Focus and Maintain Momentum

THERE'S ONLY ONE REAL "TO DO" LIST.

> Take the time and do the work to fully understand what you truly desire. The more clearly you know what it is, the more surely you can make it real.
>
> —Ralph S. Marston, Jr.[1]

Borrowed from the Japanese term for "chatter," pecha kucha has been praised as the new way to communicate in business.[2] Essentially, its main tenet is "use fewer words to say more in less time." Take the hot air out of long-winded PowerPoint presentations, for instance. According to the pecha kucha principle, you're allowed twenty slides at twenty seconds each. In under seven minutes, you say what you have to say, then sit back down. It has come to this: execu-speak lite; McBusiness talk on the run.

Is our attention span so short? The interactive mini-blog Web site known as Twitter allows for a total of 140 characters to relate your message to your network of acquaintances, but it allows unlimited access to feeds (unless someone blocks you).* The site 15SecondTV.com offers a viral marketing tool for businesses to broadcast their fifteen-second video message via mobile phone or online. It's fast entertainment at a fraction of the price. The modern belief is that hypercommunication is somehow better. It melds with the speed of the times, thereby fostering it further.

Are we just not able to focus for more than the length of a few characters or of a snapshot video? *Boston Globe* work-life columnist Maggie Jackson poses that question in an entire book on the topic of our collective distraction.[3] We are a split-screen world, nomads in a never-ending cycle of motion. We can't focus because we've never learned how. In a now oft-cited *Atlantic Monthly* article, "Is Google Making Us Stupid?"[4] Encyclopedia Britannica advisor Nicholas Carr bemoans our lack of focus. With everything at our fingertips, why should we ever hold a book, read a map, or think deeply again?

Perhaps our collective need for quick communication stems from its surplus. To field the land mines of information excess, the Oregon-based nonprofit organization Information Over-

---

*Visit www.twitter.com/hohlbaum for an example.

load Research Group was founded on the tenet that people are no longer capable of sifting through the data flying in their faces on a daily basis. The result is an overload so great we need nonprofits to steer our well-strewn attention. We require major corporations, such as the microchip company Intel, imposing "no e-mail" Fridays and "quiet-time" Tuesdays. Indeed, these measures have dramatically increased productivity while decreasing stress levels. What's shocking is the fact we need them at all.

Some companies are resorting to aggressive measures to regain worker focus. According to a 2008 survey by Chicago-based consulting firm Challenger, Gray & Christmas, 23 percent of companies have started to block social-networking sites so that employees remain focused on the job. A reported 32.7 percent claimed these sites present a drain on worker productivity.

The truth is, we *have* lost focus. A British research group at University College London conducted a first-ever longitudinal study on student online research habits. They found students rely heavily on search engines while briefly skimming articles as opposed to actually reading them. The conclusion is students display a broader lack of critical thinking skills to appropriately assess the information they collect online. Unbeknownst to many young students, a high search ranking does not indicate the information's validity. A whole new set of skills for discerning importance is required. Libraries and educational institutions are obliged to respond to the online demands of today's youth while steering them in the right direction.

In today's research environment an addendum to the age-old saying "don't believe everything you read" is required.

"Don't believe everything you read . . . on the first page of Google."

In this chapter, we will look at ways to eliminate distraction, become more selective of the activities in which we engage, and avoid information overload through skilled focus.

Principle #1: Dig Deep—Casting a Wide Net with a Singular Purpose

Typically, babies learn to crawl before they walk. Taking small steps toward the end result is essential in realizing your goals. Yet all too often we get overwhelmed by the big picture. It looks too daunting to even tackle so we distract ourselves with unimportant things to avoid the confrontation. Most often, people resort to complaining instead of focusing their energy on the task at hand. "Complaining," says Jason Womack, cofounder of an executive coaching company, "is simply the expression of not combining a person's vision of what could or should be with consistent (and often small) action steps to create the change they want to see."

Quoting an old farmer friend, copywriter John Childers says, "Never look down the row." Instead of looking at the mountain of work you have to accomplish, just start somewhere. Steadily hacking away at it bit by bit instead of looking down the entire row to some distant future accomplishment will dramatically increase your chances of success. "Just dig in," Childers suggests. "The wisdom of this is captured in the old adage 'Well begun is half done.'"

As we discussed in chapter 5, procrastination originates when our fear blocks us from doing what we know needs to happen to move to the next step. Tackling any project can be intimidating, especially if you can't see the parts that make up the whole. Break down your project into foreseeable events. If you're responsible for starting a new volunteer program, for instance, start by designing a mission statement first. What do you want to accomplish? How will this benefit the organization? You? The stakeholders? By digging deep into the meaning of what you are doing, you can help quell some of the overwhelming feelings you may have when starting something new. As Jack Canfield writes in *The Success Principles*, if you don't know where you are going, you're never going to get there.

A mission statement can be applied to any type of endeavor: whether it's starting a family, working on a work-related project, or developing a new business. Include all the things to which you are committed in your mission statement.

1. Identify the purpose of your project.
2. Remind yourself of your commitment and why it is important to you.
3. Provide reference points to ensure quality control.
4. Offer action steps to attain the goals stated in your mission statement.

A mission statement needn't be long. In fact, the term "statement" refers to its simplicity.

Rosalea Hostetler, founder and president of the Balmer Fund, Inc., attributes her forty-year commitment to preserving her hometown in Harper, Kansas, to the integrity of her straightforward mission statement: "To preserve the history, art, and culture of the prairies for future generations." Once an oasis of intellect on the prairie, the small town has become divided. "Had I not stayed focused on our mission statement," Rosalea wrote me recently, "I would have given up many times when treated unfairly, watching as they put up a six-foot fence to keep me out of our building. The powers that be razed it, vandalized it, shunned and gossiped about me for years." Despite massive community resistance, spanning from the sheriff's office to her own family, Rosalea's passion has withstood the test of time. She has saved several buildings, started a new publication, and strengthened others' resolve to stand up for what they believe in.

As with anything, keeping your commitment at the forefront of your mind saves you from wasting time on things that do not serve your purpose. Your mission statement is the sieve that helps you capture the good stuff when panning for gold. It helps you fight feelings of being overwhelmed, thereby granting you more time to focus.

Once you've written your mission statement, tack it in a conspicuous place to help you remain clear about what's important to you. When the going gets tough, you will be reminded of the reason you do what you do.

Principle #2: Pick and Choose

Information overload is not a new phenomenon, but the speed at which information lambasts us daily has changed. Consider express package delivery. What used to be an adjective has now become a verb. To "overnight" something is to send it for arrival the very next day. And, in today's info-saturated environment, sometimes even overnight is not fast enough.

Deva Hazarika and her peers at the Information Overload Research Group, before forming their company in 2007, held a workshop for professionals to discuss the issue of information overload and how it affects productivity and happiness. Her group is working toward ways to avoid workplace distraction. Deva defines information overload as a state in which "you face more pieces of information that require some response or action from you than you can deal with in the time you have available." Data elimination is one way. Picking and choosing from the sea of data is another.

It works for John Childers. To relax his overactive mind, he allows himself time to unfocus before delving back into the task at hand. He has found not fighting the information flow to be the easier route.

"If I decide I do need to totally focus on something for lengthy periods, I give myself permission to focus in and focus out, usually in fifteen- to twenty-minute increments with out-focus periods of five minutes or so." He selects the most important activity and then takes a break before doing something else.

Picking and choosing also involves prioritizing. Separate what absolutely has to get done from what you may like to do but is not a must. The temptation is often great to do the fun and easy activities first. On some days, when your focus isn't as sharp, it may even be advisable to start off easy on yourself to maintain the momentum you need. On those days, set a timer to ensure you get yourself back on track after completing the more enjoyable tasks. Sometimes fifteen minutes invested in pure delight can sustain your energy through the more difficult tasks later in your day.

Principle #3: Get Specific, Make a Plan

Focus is an elusive thing if you don't have a clear idea what you should be focusing on in the first place.

Sports psychology consultant Jason Selk, director of counseling and sport psychology at St. Louis–based Enhanced Performance, Inc., says the number-one challenge for people in gaining focus is their lack of details. When he consults for the St. Louis Cardinals, he asks each player what his specific strength is, then asks him to focus on just that one thing. The same thing applies to Joe Officeworker, who's so frazzled by the daily demands he has no idea where to look first. Identifying the specific thing you need to focus on helps eliminate distraction considerably. Much like prioritizing, boiling down the most important aspect of your day can bring you into laserlike focus. Instead of considering the overwhelming variables, ask yourself: "What's the first thing I need to focus on to be successful?"

The second step is to create a mental training program. Visualize yourself already at your goal. Believe it or not, semantics matter. Formulating your thoughts in a negative manner will automatically signal to your brain that you should concentrate on the thing behind the "not." For instance, consider that yoga class you know is good for you, but stretches your limits. If you go into it thinking, "I'm *not* going to think this is hard today!" your mind will think the *opposite* due to the negative formulation. Reiterate your goals in the positive. Think, "Today, this is easy! I enjoy yoga with ease and grace." Use the present tense to bring the belief into the here and now.

In terms of your relationship with time, ask yourself what is the exact opposite of time-starved? What would it be like to be time-rich? Imagine yourself with all the time in the world. What's the one thing you need to focus on that will give you that feeling? Perhaps it means blocking out an entire chunk of your day in which you do not schedule anything at all. It may sound scary, but setting aside a moment to appreciate time will help your relationship to it.

To regain good relations with your calendar, practice your mental training program daily through visualization. Keep those negative thoughts in check by reminding yourself of what it feels like to live in a time-rich world.

Principle #4: Trigger Points

Identify your trigger points, such as when your boss asks you into her office at 5 P.M. on a Friday to dump that project on you due Monday at 9 A.M., or when your unreliable friend leaves you in the lurch—again.

If you think about it, we spend a great deal of our day managing our trigger points. We spin thoughts in our mind that suck more energy from us than we even realize. The neighbor's parked too close to your driveway again. The trash collector forgot to empty your foulest garbage can for the third time. What can you do to alleviate these triggers?

There is peace in acceptance as well as in action. Listing all the things that preoccupy you can be tremendously helpful in identifying what drives you to distraction. Include everything that irks you, down to the tiniest details, such as the color of your office walls. Next to each item, mark what steps you could take to improve the situation. Sometimes taking a simple action can free up a great deal of energy and focus for the things that truly matter.

Oftentimes, we can find simple ways to circumvent those triggers. Ciaran Blumenfeld, mom of four children and owner of an online children's clothing store, used to hate backtracking. Being late is a nightmare in her mind so every time she'd get lost in the car and have to make a U-turn, she would stress out even more than before she got lost. One day she invested in a GPS unit. What used to waste a lot of time and energy has virtually been eliminated. Now her husband, who is directionally challenged, no longer minds the gentle prodding to take a left or right because it's not coming from his wife. On the rare occasion that the family is in a real hurry, she drives. Ciaran identified an easily remedied trigger and dealt with it.

Living in harmony with your surroundings is crucial to your concentration. You may not be able to control who your boss is or how your spouse drives, but you can certainly learn ways to live side by side without annoyance.

Principle #5: Forgiveness

Forgiveness is a powerful tool in building a solid relationship with time. What beauty manufacturers don't want you to know is you've earned your marks. They want to shame you into believing you should look or be a certain way. The truth is, you are the only *you* there is, a unique human being with characteristics all your own. Forgiving yourself for your own humanity lets you take a leap forward in knowing everything has a time and place.

New York–based communications consultant and certified coach Lauree Ostrofsky says forgiveness is a big step toward learning how to do things one at a time. "If I'm working on something, I often feel guilty about not doing something else. I know it sounds silly, but it's like each to-do has a voice begging me to choose it. When I make my choice, I'm letting one of them down. The key to focus is (1) being honest about what you really want to do, and (2) forgiving yourself for not being able to do it all so you can just do that one thing really well."

How else is forgiveness helpful in maintaining our momentum? Consider the time you spend fretting about what you haven't done. This is much like Principle #1, where we learned that looking at the mountain of things before you can lead to paralysis. The PowerPoint presentation, the monthly report due yesterday, and the Girl Scout meeting at 5 P.M. are dueling priorities. We like to call our lives a balancing or juggling act, but do we really want to join the circus of metaphors for trying to accomplish the impossible?

We all want to lead happy, fulfilled lives, yet many of us feel hindered by all the to-dos given voice by our own minds. Forgiving ourselves for our inability to be everywhere at once is crucial to our focus. We've all had moments like Michael Keaton's character in the movie *Multiplicity*: An overworked father whose guilt over spending so little time with his family leads him to partake in a cloning experiment. He creates three copies of himself. From weak to sinister, each clone represents a part of his own psyche. I don't know about you, but can you imagine having three more of you running around? Before reaching for the test tube, give forgiveness a try.

Principle #6: Create the Space

As you've learned by now, there's no such thing as time management since you can't manage something you can't control.
But you can manage what you do in the time you have and, for
that matter, *where* you do it, too. You have some influence, for
instance, on the work space you inhabit. If you work in an open
office setting and your cube mate's phone chatter distracts you,
use earplugs while writing that report. Surround yourself with
beauty. Put a lovely plant on your desk, or pictures of your
loved ones and photos that inspire you.

Amateur travel podcaster Chris Christensen creates his own
space to record his shows away from the distraction of television and family. "Those who suffer from Continuous Partial
Attention (CPA) call it 'multitasking.' We can do two things at
once and do it well—or so we say," he related to me one day.
But he soon realized his lack of focus was keeping him from
doing the best job he could. "Now all my podcasting takes
place in a room in the second story of our house away from
the TV in the family room."

Allowing space for your own creativity to unfold assists tremendously in maintaining your momentum. We all know the
feeling of being motivated when we start something new. We're
full of energy, excited about the future, and genuinely grateful
for the new experience. But joy can quickly turn to burden if
you don't allow your new idea to breathe. Granting yourself
space to maneuver reduces stress while feeding your progress.

Positive-psychology coach Caroline Adams Miller came up
with a cost-effective way to save her time and her own sanity
by staying at hotels near her house when she needed to work.

"One year I had to write two books on brutal deadlines while working full time and raising three kids," she says. "I found that doing Priceline bids to local hotels is the most inexpensive and wonderful way ever to carve out private time to reflect." She routinely bids on nearby hotels for three nights away. For less than $150, she can have the four-star hotel experience, become more productive, and get the rest she needs.

In this exercise, create the space for you to focus in. If you know you have several pending projects, design your surroundings to match your needs. If working at night suits you best, it might mean making an arrangement with your boss that you can work from home instead of dealing with the daytime distractions of the office. Or carve out space for yourself by literally getting away from your immediate surroundings and going elsewhere. Concentration requires space. Make sure yours uplifts rather than distracts you.

Principle #7: Distraction Elimination

Dwight D. Eisenhower once said, "What is important is seldom urgent and what is urgent is seldom important." The result of that statement was the emergence of the Eisenhower principle, a management concept later made popular by Dr. Stephen Covey in his book 7 *Habits of Highly Effective People*.

The Eisenhower principle suggests that you separate urgent matters from important ones. *Urgent matters* typically involve issues relating to the achievement of someone else's goals, an uncomfortable challenge that requires immediate attention. *Important matters* relate to the accomplishment of your own goals. They need to be added to your calendar to keep you on a suitable time line. By matching your goals with the appropriate milestones, you can harmonize them with the time you have available to you.

Sometimes matters are urgent *and* important, critical actions you have put off or ignored completely until it's almost too late, such as filing your income taxes on April 15. Other times you have matters that are urgent and unimportant, which are mere interruptions in your day, such as the telephone ringing off the hook. Nonurgent important activities require your attention over the long-term—essential activities to achieve your objectives, such as running every day to train for a marathon. Nonurgent, nonimportant things, such as Internet gambling, may be fun, but serve only to distract, not foster, your higher purpose.

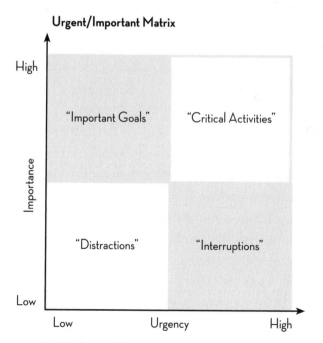

Source: www.MindTools.com, © Mind Tools Ltd, 2009.

Essentially, you can toss out most of what falls in the lower left quadrant. You can manage the lower right quadrant, such as errant children invading your home office space or nonstop cubicle visitors, by setting distinct boundaries. These two lower quadrants are where you have to make the most effort to eliminate sidetracking distractions and interruptions. As with tiny triggers, it's often the little things that have the greatest impact. Removing them from our routine at given intervals ensures greater attention to what really matters.

The upper two quadrants should receive the majority of our attention, as it is here that we strive toward our ultimate purpose. While it is not always possible, get into the habit of allowing room for unexpected urgent and important matters to crop up in your day. Scheduling events too close together gives you no breathing room and invites a domino effect if you don't provide a buffer zone for unforeseeable events.

When Shaun Dakin worked as an executive for FedEx, he learned four similar principles of management that saved him time in prioritizing. According to FedEx founder Fred Smith's managerial philosophy of the four Ds, you either *do, delegate, delete,* or *delay.* "FedEx is a very action-oriented organization," Shaun wrote. "Fred made it clear that there were things that you did *now* (respond to customers) and things that needed to be delayed (more information needed) or simply killed (deleted)." He successfully implements this strategy today as CEO and founder of the National Political Do Not Contact Registry. Combining both the Eisenhower principle and the four Ds, you can get more clarity about what needs to be done now, later, or not at all.

Principle #8: Honor Set-Up Time

In her book *Unwinding the Clock*, Swedish physicist Bodil Jönsson contemplates our relationship with time in an ever-demanding world that allows little space for thought. She cautions us not to forget the importance of taking time to think.

She delineates between divided time and undivided time. To explain the difference, consider the example of summer vacation. We all remember having endless summer days as kids. Our free time felt endless because we had no perceived time line as we did during the school year. There were few, if any, scheduled activities, and time seemed to float away from our day-to-day existence. We experienced undivided time. It wasn't segmented into smaller bits called day camp, two-week trip or, if you were unlucky, summer school. Attuned to our more natural rhythms, we relied on external cues such as the sun setting to remind us it was time to go home.

Similarly, if you look at the most enjoyable vacations you have had as an adult, it hasn't necessarily been a lack of activity that made them so wonderful. It had more to do with the lack of division in your time. You reunited with your circadian beat, befriending the clock in a new way. You invited in spontaneity—without forethought or a moment to fret with built-up expectations. You simply lived in the moment, unharnessed from the rigors of divided time.

Jönsson talks about the much-neglected "set-up time" required to do just about anything. Set-up time refers to the time it takes you to organize your thoughts, papers, and schedule to get started on a specific task. Set-up time varies, depending on the task at hand. A circus clown will require a certain amount of set-up time before performing his act. He wasn't born with makeup on his face, nor does he customarily wear a red nose when not in the ring. A waitress needs another type of set-up time before her shift—filling saltshakers, replenishing supplies, and cleaning are necessary before the restaurant's doors can open. Set-up time is a part of the whole. Without it, you're a jumble of thoughts and emotions without direction.

Filmmaker, producer, and screenwriter Nancy Fulton values her set-up time as much as she does the act of creating itself. She never simply sits down and starts writing without giving a project her best thinking. In fact, sometimes she will take months before she writes a single word. Then, once the idea has ripened in her mind, she can pound out an entire screenplay in a very short time because she is telling a story she already knows well. She dreams the story first, until it is mature, then she captures it on the page to later translate to the screen. In order to complete the process and do her job well, she requires set-up time. "I must allow my subconscious to cook before I write or it all goes horribly wrong," she told me in a telephone interview. By honoring her set-up time, Nancy can write an entire screenplay in a matter of weeks. In fact, the original screenplay for her latest film, *No Better Friend*, which has garnered interest from Judd Nelson to play the starring role, was written in a week. Her story is proof of the power of slow. You can often achieve more by *doing* less.

Whatever your position, you require a certain amount of set-up time for your various duties. Consider how much set-up time you need for each activity. It might take you longer to put away groceries than someone else because you have to walk three flights of stairs to your apartment. Picking up the dry cleaning might be a snap because you live right down the street from the nearest shop. Set-up time is a highly individualized aspect of your relationship with time. It's ever-changing as well because it adapts to your circumstances as they adjust, too.

Even the time of day may influence the length of time it takes to do something. Are you a morning person? Your set-up time will be shorter in the morning than in the late afternoon. Do you work nights? Most likely, the timing of your set-up time is different from most. Regardless of what the clock says, everyone has his or her own rhythm. Find yours, and remember to include the time it takes to prepare yourself before setting off from point A to point B.

Principle #9: The Rule of Thirty

Contributing to the annual $5.7 billion earned in the yoga industry, the New York yoga studio Namaste New York specializes in yoga for stressed-out executives. Offering them a moment of solace in their busy routines, the studio helps Wall Street workers and others to maintain balance in their otherwise tumultuous lives. It's an encouraging trend as the impact of exercise is not only felt for the individual but quite possibly for the entire U.S. economy. Who would you rather have on the trading floor? Mr. Nine-Cups-of-Java ready for a heart attack at age forty or a well-stretched, grounded sixty-year-old?

The long-term effects of regular exercise are well documented. A recent study on exercise and mental fitness shows a link between negative fitness levels and brain atrophy in early

Alzheimer's patients. Those patients with a higher peak oxygen consumption experienced less brain shrinkage than those with lower fitness levels.[5] Dr. William Haskell at Stanford University School of Medicine has been integral in establishing physical fitness guidelines for Americans. In the Physical Activity Guidelines Advisory Committee Report for 2008, Dr. Haskell and his advisors suggest thirty minutes of exercise five days a week to maintain your weight. According to the report, consistent exercise can reduce heart disease, high blood pressure, depression, and the effects of aging.

Dr. David G. Lee, director of the Georgia-based Wellness Revolution Clinics, recommends taking thirty minutes *before breakfast* to gather your focus for the day. He suggests breaking up the time into three equally timed activities: 1) meditation or prayer; 2) self-reflection; and 3) exercise. During your meditative moment, think about the things for which you are grateful. Commune with your own spirit. Next, reflect on all the things you accomplished the day before. Be proud of your achievements. Acknowledge yourself. Lastly, take ten minutes to stretch, move about, or do a few yoga poses, which will help spur on your metabolism for a great start to the day.

Incorporating the rule of thirty into your daily routine will improve your mental and physical well-being.

Principle #10: Meditation

Physical fitness isn't the only factor in keeping focused. Mental agility is equally important. Jumpy minds and jumbled thinking often prevail in our 24/7 lives. The constant distractions, interruptions, dueling priorities, and seemingly endless to-do lists shake us up, cause stress, and lower our productivity. The result is attention through a prism, spewing our gaze in myriad directions.

Meditation has a proven effect to calm the mind. You might be thinking it is an impossible task to sit still for even a minute. But research has proven that as little as twenty minutes of daily meditation steadies our attention. Dr. Richard J. Davidson, Antoine Lutz, and their colleagues at the University of Wisconsin have studied the effects of meditation on brain function. There are indications that a short program of mindful meditation may actually have a positive impact on brain and immune functions.[6] Meditation clearly adds to people's well-being and affects attentive brain functions.

There are two prevalent forms of meditation: focused attention meditation (FA) in which you stare at, say, a candle flame or focus only on your breath as Buddhist monks do; and open monitoring meditation (OM), in which you remain in a monitoring state of awareness without focusing on any specific object. The idea is if we become aware of our mental state, we will improve our ability to transform negative emotional and cognitive habits.

Getting into an alpha state is a prerequisite for meditation. The alpha brain wave state is the state in which we are most relaxed and our best learning takes place. Avil Beckford, president of Ambeck Enterprise, walked me through the seven-step process one day. Get into a comfortable position. Close your eyes and release your thoughts as best you can. Take several deep breaths by extending your belly outward, then inward. With your eyes still closed, allow them to look upward to the spot between your eyebrows. As you begin to feel a slight pressure in your eyes, silently count backward from ten to one. By the time you reach one, you have also reached alpha. Your meditation can begin.

No one knows the benefits of meditation better than psychotherapist and former multitasker Michelle Bersell. She used to squeeze so much into a day that she'd be left frazzled and exhausted. Watching television without simultaneously folding laundry, reading the paper, or paying bills seemed to her like a waste of time. The thought of closing her eyes and emptying her mind sounded like torture for even a minute, much less for twenty. One day a friend told her to try it right after she woke up in the morning for five minutes. Lying on her back, she managed to maintain stillness. It was a welcome change from her hectic mornings, and she quite enjoyed feeling centered for once. After a week, she noticed she was able to lie still for ten minutes before getting restless. By month's end she was up to sixty minutes at a time. She also noticed how her focus had become sharper. She started paying attention to the little things when going for a walk in the woods or doing mundane tasks. Her heart was flooded with joy at the simplicity of it all. In short, she had discovered the power of slow and the beauty its equilibrium brings.

Final Word

In this chapter, we looked at how to stop your focus from slipping through your fingers like grains of sand. Use a mission statement to clarify your vision; avoid information overload by picking and choosing where your energy will go; remember that life is in the details, so you need to be specific about where you will put your focus; identify your triggers and take steps to remedy them; forgive yourself for your inability to split your attention effectively; manifest space for your creativity; eliminate distraction by determining what's important and urgent; leave room for set-up time; apply the rule of thirty-minute movement daily; and calm your mind with meditative moments. You're almost there. The next phase is to tell others what to do so you can do what you do best. But that, my friend, is stuff for the next chapter.

10

Delegation: Ten Ways to Do What You Do Best So Others Can, Too

I can't change the direction of the wind, but I can adjust my sails to always reach my destination.

—Jimmy Dean

The progress of the do-it-yourself movement can be found in home-improvement stores across the nation. If you've ever lurked in the saw-dusty aisles on a Saturday morning, you'll see weekend warriors filling their shopping carts with all kinds of power tools, paint cans, and primers. The pioneer spirit lives on within our own four walls as we explore new frontiers in our own domain. Self-reliance, or pulling ourselves up by our own bootstraps, is the basis of who we are as Americans. So at first glance, delegation can appear to be the very opposite.

Delegation is about moving from doing things yourself to getting things done through others. It is a skill set just like knowing how to speak Swahili, doing needlepoint, pole jumping, or digging holes for fence posts. But ask people what they hate doing most besides public speaking, and you'll surely hear them say "managing other people." Delegation is not a talent you are born with, so why then do some people seem to have an innate ability to ask others to do things for them without guilt or strain? These people honed their skills through experience. The good news is you can learn how to delegate, too. It involves trust, instinct, knowledge, and communication.

You may struggle with letting go, wanting to control the outcome, and feeling as if you are the only one who can "do it right." In fact, the do-it-yourself philosophy rests on the premise that it will get done right *only* if you do it yourself. This type of thinking kills the power of delegation and your relationship with time because the truth is no one can do everything all the time. To truly live the power of slow, you need to give over, not take over.

According to Brian Denis Egan at the business training company Global Knowledge, managers either delegate or suffocate.[1] As supervisors of others, managers have the primary task of delegating to others. It's about pooling resources and having the best person do the job, whether it is in their job description or not. It's also about monitoring tasks to be sure they are done in a timely manner.

Delegation is not just reserved for the executive office, however. It is a vital component in living the power of slow. Consider yourself the executive of your life. You too can learn the skill of delegating where it counts. As you farm out tasks to those who can do them best, you free up time and energy to do what *you* do best. What happens when you are overloaded with too many things on your to-do list? You rush around, expecting yourself to complete everything on the same day without realizing your potential because of overlapping demands. The key is to surround yourself with self-motivated delegates. By doing so, you will save days of time otherwise wasted on activities best left to the experts who enjoy doing what you may not.

Let's look at a real-life example. A mother of four, Deborah Morehead was working full time as director of strategic planning and development for a marketing promotions company when she realized the only way she could align her children's schedules with her own was to delegate tasks to a neighborhood teenager. The girl would pick up one of her children after school and take him to soccer practice. She also ran errands, such as picking up the dry cleaning and going grocery shopping. In exchange for her once-a-week duties, the teen, who was also a member of the swim team, was allowed to swim in Deborah's pool in the early mornings. In the winter months, Deborah gave her SAT tutoring and résumé assistance to pay the teen back for her time during the week. Delegation can be easy, even joyful, if you match the right duties with the right delegates.

The following chart will give you an overview of the issues we will discuss in this chapter.

Why We Delegate	Why We Don't Delegate
• Reduces your workload.	• It's too time-consuming to explain; easier to just do it yourself.
• Frees up time to complete other tasks.	• You think you can do it better.
• Enhances your efficiency.	• Your authority is diminished.
• Allows others to develop their skill set.	• Control and risk aversion. You want to have control and avoid risk.
• May produce faster results.	• You don't want to look lazy or commanding.
• Enhances your leadership skills.	• You fear someone might show you up by doing it better.

How to Delegate	How Not to Delegate
• Provide your delegate with the necessary authority and control to complete the job; follow up appropriately.	• Follow up incessantly or not at all.
• Be specific when explaining expected results.	• Farm out only the simple tasks.
• Enhance engagement by explaining the "big picture" and why the person is doing the task ("Your creating mailing lists enables the company to reach more customers").	• Expect others to be perfect or approach things the way you would ("I expect you to do it a certain way, but I'm not going to tell you how").
• Share the recognition with your team members.	• Take all the credit. Leave everyone else in the dust.

How to Delegate	How Not to Delegate
• Celebrate your "wins"; reward appropriately.	• Overwhelm your delegates with too much responsibility.
• Trust your delegates.	• Mismatch set expectations with your behavior.

Source: Adapted from Corporate Trendsetters by permission

In this chapter we will look at ways to allow yourself to excel in your realm of expertise while having others do the same. Delegation is not about shirking responsibility, but about asking each person to live up to her potential while you live up to your own.

According to business consultant Kevin Eikenberry, delegation is not about you, but about others. It is not about dumping, but about developing other people's potential. He cautions about the pitfalls of delegation if done incorrectly, including delegating too much too soon or too little too late.[2] The principles below will address when to delegate, how to go about it, and what to avoid in the process. We will look at delegation both within your organization and when outsourcing to others.

Principle #1: The Top Ten Won't Dos

We all have things in our lives that we dislike doing, such as cleaning windows or mowing the lawn. They are items in our day we'd prefer to ignore, yet they have to get done nonetheless. Pushing them off doesn't work in the long run, as we learned in chapter 5. Procrastination wastes more time than if you were to simply get it done. To face the tasks head-on, tap into the power of delegation by identifying those things you would like to hand off to someone else, not necessarily because you despise the work, but because you know someone else will appreciate doing the task either for the financial reward or the satisfaction it brings.

Frenzy often stems from having too much on your plate at once. Delegation is an integral part of alleviating urgency. Remember, this book is about improving your relationship with time; obviously, erasing items from your packed schedule will help ease the strain of feeling time-crunched.

Make a list of the top ten things you know someone else could do. Call it your list of won't dos. Think of people in your circle who might help you complete these tasks because they're better at them than you. It is a misperception to think you have to do everything yourself. We live in community with others. We are here to support each other to be the best we can be. It might mean having your kids organize your checks by number or raking the leaves. It might involve hiring a window-washing service for your building. Whatever the task, you can divide what you can do from what you cannot on your list.

If you live in a multiperson household, gather everyone around the kitchen table for a heart-to-heart talk about which tasks each person will be responsible for completing. If you have children, couple age-appropriate chores with earning an allowance. It will teach children money-management skills while instilling in them a sense of ownership. You will have less to do, and everyone learns something from the experience. If you live alone, seek out hired help or barter with someone else. The neighbor mows the lawn; you host the block party. Your friend's son takes the recycling to the dump; you teach him how to play baseball. Depending on your situation, bartering might not be the best solution for you. If you are able, hire someone to complete a task to free up your time, as long as the person you've hired is most suitable for the job.

Principle #2: Build Your Delegation Using the Trust Test

Networking is an important part of the delegation process. How do you go about finding your delegates in the first place? No one lives in a vacuum. In fact, being around other people can contribute to your longevity. According to Stephen Post and Jill Neimark, people who surround themselves with community and kindness tend to live longer.[3] Acts of kindness impact your well-being, so if you are struggling with the idea of letting go, remember you may be committing the kindest act ever by asking someone to help you.

It is a well-documented fact that generativity, or the concern for people of the next generation, leads to lower mortality rates. According to many recent studies, the elderly who volunteer their time tend to live longer. Frequent volunteering has been found to dramatically reduce depression and other mental health issues in the elderly. Asking an elderly person in your neighborhood to contribute to you is not only an act of delegation, but an act of kindness, too.

Building your delegation might take time on the front end, but it will save you time in the long run. Depending on your requirements, you may be able to ask for referrals from friends. Social-networking sites such as LinkedIn.com, Xing.com, and

Facebook offer a plethora of connections, while eLance.com offers all kinds of freelancers to assist you in your business needs. It is always best to review people's profiles, ask for references, and conduct your due diligence before hiring someone. Part of the process is trial and error because you never really know whether someone will work out or not until you try. Be prepared to occasionally miss the mark and to find yourself having to try something new.

Delegation has everything to do with trust. In this exercise of building your delegation, conduct the trust test in your mind. Ask yourself if you would trust this person to deposit a thousand-dollar check in the bank for you. If the answer is yes, he's the right man for the job. If the answer is no, move on.

Principle #3: Farm Out Guilt-Free

If you are battling with yourself about farming out work to other people, remember the win-win scenario you are creating. You know the other person will benefit from completing the task on your behalf; whether you are paying them, assigning them a new challenge, or granting them a sense of accomplishment, everyone benefits from the division of labor. You save time. Your delegates learn something. Your win equals theirs.

Attorney and radio show host Elizabeth Potts Weinstein handles her guilt-free delegation by assigning not only tasks but entire roles. She calls it "complete delegation" because the delegate receives a full job description. Instead of getting a personal shopper to get the supplies on her grocery list, she has hired someone who handles the entire family inventory. Periodically, her personal shopper goes through her supplies, noting what needs replenishing from the master inventory list. Elizabeth applies the same principles to her finance radio program in which her assistant is now her assistant producer, in charge of program management and interview bookings. Instead of receiving random e-mails with various tasks, her assistant has a clear-cut position within which she maneuvers beautifully.

Guilt-free outsourcing empowers not only the farmer, but the delegate. Establishing concise guidelines may require some time up front, but the rewards you will reap are long lasting and time saving indeed. If you get stuck, refer back to chapter 8 on expectation management to learn how to provide clear instructions to your delegate.

Principle #4: Empowerment Project

Empowering your delegates leads to higher retention rates. According to a recent survey by the American Management Association, 84 percent of those surveyed who called their boss "kind" planned to stay at their jobs a long time compared to only 47 percent who called their boss "a bully."[4] Empowerment includes acknowledging people on a regular basis for the work they do, offering them the tools and guidance to do their best, and providing rewards for a job well done.

The saying "Good people are hard to find" may have some truth to it, but it is equally important to remember good people can be developed. That is, you reap what you sow. Investing in your delegates is as important as selecting the right clay to mold. When you find a promising candidate, you will want to do everything in your power to keep them. If you've ever been in business, you'll know the truth of the saying "You're only as good as the team that supports you."

Alma Candelaria, former deputy director of the Office of Compliance for the U.S. House of Representatives, attributes her greatest career successes to understanding the essential nature of delegation. It is about empowerment and reaching your highest potential together, not alone.

"What I learned most through delegation is that we are smarter as a whole than as a single person. I personally had severe perfectionist tendencies. I delegated stingily until I finally realized what I was doing," she admitted. "I was hampering others' growth. By not being a hovering delegator, I learned to develop more trust. I was able to better assess team strengths and weaknesses and thus better assign and sequence assignments to capture everyone's strengths. It also gave me a broader global perspective to help staff grow developmentally."

For this exercise, design a periodic meeting with each of the people you rely on. It might be a quick phone chat or a longer face-to-face meeting. Tell them what you like about what they have done. Praise them for their strengths. A motivated delegate is a happy one who will most likely work even harder to maintain your trust.

Principle #5: Monitoring and Mentoring, Not Nagging and Micromanaging

As we have seen, doing a dump-and-run won't work to keep others motivated. Monitoring and mentoring your fledglings is part and parcel of the delegation process. Understanding how it works is best done by way of example.

Publishers Weekly book review editor Rose Fox works with dozens of freelance writers. She only hires the best and has "ruthlessly pruned" those who don't meet deadlines or quality standards. Once writers make the cut and join her team, she builds loyalty through mutual trust and respect. When she first started working as a freelance journalist, her pride and perfectionism made her wary of outsourcing until an arm injury forced her to rely on transcriptionists. She soon found that talented people could provide top-notch work and save her hours of typing. Now recovered, she still outsources all her transcription. With every assignment, she clearly defines her expectations and then lets her team loose. Trusting them to deliver good work on time lets her focus on doing her own job well. "Micromanaging is a waste of my time," she explained. "If someone needs nagging, I need to replace them with someone who doesn't need nagging." It's as simple as that.

As a partner with Yes & Company, Rita Reneaux agrees that micromanaging does not serve anyone. She recommends being prudent about the person you choose, then making sure that he or she understands the assignment and has it in writing. She underscores the importance of remaining available as a resource to the person for questions, ideas, and influence. Monitoring does not mean hovering, so be careful that you give the person free rein while still checking in periodically to assure everyone's still moving toward the project's completion.

As we have addressed elsewhere, information overload is prevalent in our 24/7 business world. Peter Luiks, a former CEO of various companies and an ex-program manager for the U.S. defense industry, advises protecting people from information overload by encouraging personal responsibility. He suggests giving them enough leverage and trust to get the job done. "Build people up, don't tear them down," he said. "Managers are there to be used." Having managed projects involving tens of thousands of people, Peter suggests personalizing your relationships with your direct delegates and encouraging them to do the same. "Remember birthdays, the names of their spouses, and other personal information. It makes people feel special and appreciated." Taking personal responsibility and being a mentor are fulfilling activities. While you may think mentoring is a time-consuming activity, by doing so you are actually transforming your relationship to the world around you by morphing your position into a very accepted leadership role. You will be free to spend time doing the things you do best, thereby changing your relationship with time itself. Embrace it. Delegation reinforces your importance as a role model while you are motivating and stimulating others.

Leslie Shreve, owner of Focus Consulting, is a productivity expert who teaches people how to properly delegate by recommending that delegators quiz their teams on a periodic basis. Questions such as "What steps might you take to complete this assignment?" and "What do you envision will come next?" help your delegates become independent thinkers. Much like when helping a child with homework, it is important to foster the learning process by not giving the answers, however tempting that might be. Asking pointed questions will vastly contribute to your delegates' growth and help correct their course in the event they are going down the wrong path.

Mentoring plays a large role in leadership. Guidance with a gentle hand instead of a cracking whip will save you a lot of time, motivate your delegates, and keep you within the scope of resources you earmarked from the beginning.

For this exercise, you will need to formulate a few monitoring questions for your team. Keep them simple and to the point without a hidden agenda. Monitoring means checking in, not checking up on people.

Principle #6: Toss Out the Blame Game

We all make mistakes once in a while. Assigning blame to people doesn't work. So when things go awry, it's important to get to the root causes by pointing out what happened versus what people did wrong. It also requires being accountable for your part in the situation.

Consider the following statements: "You didn't fax the report on time. That's why we're in this mess!" or "The information was not transferred in a timely manner. We need to improve our processes to be sure that does not happen again. What can we do differently next time?"

Avoid "you" sentences because in crisis people automatically hear blame in your voice. "You did this" and "you did that" are not positive statements. They are past-based remarks that only hinder present and future communications. Address what happened, not who did or did not do something. Offer immediate, forward-thinking solutions to avoid the same conundrum in the future. Look at what damage you may have sustained and address the implications. Use mistakes as opportunities to improve the process. You can't have processes without people so be clear what you expect from them in the future. Statements such as "Going forward, here's what I suggest we do . . ." have a proactive tone that sets people into motion instead of placing them in a state of paralysis and fear.

U.S. president Harry S. Truman had a sign on his desk: "The Buck Stops Here." Instead of passing the buck, he was reminded of his commitment to accept responsibility for whatever came his way. In a similar vein, this principle of tossing out the blame game requires you to take on personal responsibility. Saying, "I am responsible for the choices I make" is an empowering perspective. Instead of seeing yourself as the victim of your delegates, realize you chose to work with them in this manner in the first place. There is no room for blame in delegation. It will only get in the way of finding the solution to your challenges.

To apply this principle, consider where the buck stops. If it's not with you, where does it stop, then?

Principle #7: Requirements Test

What you delegate is as important as *how* you do it. Smart delegators identify their needs and hand-select how they will be fulfilled. Are you just making it up or do you really need someone else to vacuum out your car every week? Answer the question: Does this serve me and the other person? What would happen if I did not engage this person to help me?

Remember delegation is not about dumping, but about seeking out the best person for the job. Sometimes outsourcing something you can do best yourself can backfire, so you need to be selective. Thinking you don't have the time to do something is not the best strategy for deciding which duties to pass on to someone else.

Sort through the most important tasks at hand. As your seniority grows, you may have to take on tasks that fit your position rather than your preference. As you progress, you will find that priorities begin to shift. Keep a close watch on how the priorities of your project unfold, then delegate accordingly to ensure the highest quality outcome.

Lisa Murray, an excellent writer in her own right, approached several freelancers for help with some writing for her Web site. She wanted to concentrate on building her business instead of being in the midst of it so she thought farming out some work would be to her advantage. She quickly learned, however, that delegation can go awry if you delegate the wrong things. The first freelancer delivered suboptimal quality, and while the second was much better, Lisa spent so much time writing out directives that she could have done the writing assignment herself. In the end, she learned delegating involves good planning. She chose to delegate other tasks to free up the time required to expand her services.

Principle #8: Balancing Between Controlling and Letting Go

Delegation requires a balancing act between autonomy and control. You want your delegates to soar while keeping an invisible tether on them in the event they get lost in the clouds. Micromanaging is a bad idea as it undermines the trust you've worked so hard to attain. Laurent Duperval, who runs his own communications company in Montreal, Canada, offers a surefire way to resist asking for incessant updates by agreeing on milestones before the project begins. "Whenever you feel the uncontrollable urge to get a status update before the next scheduled milestone," he says, "make a written list of twenty reasons why you absolutely have to get the information now. Review the list and if there are five reasons that will cause the failure of the project, then proceed. Otherwise, give your team the opportunity to stand up to the challenge on its own."

The balance between control and independence can be had if you develop milestones. As Laurent mentions, they should be agreed upon before starting the project. You can maintain a level of awareness while allowing your delegates' abilities to unfurl by following these balancing principles:

1. Define the job, objectives, and workload, and divide them into doable pieces.
2. Choose the correct person for the job at hand.
3. Alert the delegate of your plans in writing.
4. Manage the process.
5. Upon project completion, assess the results with praise and a constructive review.

Milestones are important for checking in, but it is equally important to give your delegates a semblance of independence. After struggling with the balance between autonomy and control, Trista Harris, executive director of the Headwaters Foundation for Justice, realized she needed to delegate the objective and not the process itself. "When I first started delegating projects without step-by-step instructions," she wrote, "I was amazed at the final results that I got back. New perspectives solved problems that I didn't even know I had and people really shine when you don't hamstring them with a ton of directions."

Assessment is a big part of delegation because it helps you evaluate the success rate of your project. You will need to check in on two levels: with yourself and with your delegates. To check in with yourself, review what you have done to empower your delegates and what you might do in the future to improve communication, knowledge transfer, and monitoring. Gary Rosensteel, who runs a startup advisory firm, quickly learned that actually accomplishing his goals was much more important than how he went about it. "I learned in my first days of management to concentrate on achieving objectives on time and within budget to the satisfaction of the 'customer' rather than put time into how people did their job. You have to allow people the room to express their own style."

The best way to find out how *you* did in your task delegation is to ask during the monitoring phase and then, later, at the end of the process. Assessing without judgment requires tactful communication and the willingness to give and receive constructive criticism.

For this principle, you will need to institute a system of checks and balances for yourself. Are you letting go enough while maintaining an overview? How much time do you spend balancing the two? If it is more than the amount of time it would take to complete the task yourself, you need to reevaluate the roles you are delegating.

Principle #9: Leave the Clones at Home

It may take you a while to realize no one will do things the way you do. Deborah Morehead might have handled the errands in a different order than the teen she engaged to do them for her, but the end result was the same. The dry cleaning and her son still got picked up, and the grocery shopping got done, too. We all have our own particular set of idiosyncrasies. Delegation is not about hiring a clone. You want people to manage the task to the best of their ability and to your satisfaction. Unreasonable expectations are some of the biggest time-wasters as you fret about things you cannot influence. You can make suggestions, requests, and give clear guidelines: The rest is up to your delegates to accomplish.

Executive coach Leila Bulling Towne used to direct corporate training at a global Internet media company in San Francisco. In her own practice, one of the greatest challenges her senior executive clients have is learning the difference between merely managing and leading. A great manager is a great delegator, which makes him or her a great leader. No talent pool will yield your twin, nor would you want it to. Differences lead to enhancements, not detractions, in your life. Allow for people to do the job the way that works best for them. As long as they are meeting time lines and milestones, it doesn't matter whether they pick up the groceries or the dry cleaning first.

In this exercise, acknowledge the different skill sets you possess compared to your delegates. Realize you have engaged them because of the enhancement they bring to your support network. Celebrate the diversity!

Principle #10: Foster Loyalty Through Celebration

Speaking of celebration, a job well done is worth a moment of reward. Praise can come in little ways such as a nice handwritten note or a kind word. Match your delegates' reward with the scope of their work. If they successfully completed an assignment on time, or even early, organize recognition in your corporate newsletter or, at the very least, in front of other people. When one of my consultants volunteered for an assignment without extra pay, I took her out for lunch as a thank-you for her extra effort. Loyalty can be easily fostered by acknowledging people along the way.

Marika Flatt, owner of PR by the Book, understands the importance of celebrating her team's wins. It's not only uplifting for her employees, but it also adds fun to the workday routine. She and her husband, who is also co-owner, occasionally throw a party at their home or take the team members out to dinner after a particularly successful campaign. Because the publicists all happen to be female, Marika likes to create special girls' nights as team-building exercises. Through her positive working relationship, she has fostered a sense of loyalty that inspires her teammates to work even harder while they remember the difference they make every day.

In this exercise, think of ways you can celebrate your delegates' wins. It might be as simple as remembering their birthdays or doing a write-up on your company blog. Win builds upon win. If you take time to spotlight success, you'll get more of it by the sheer loyalty you create.

Final Word

Delegation is one of the best time-saving devices, if you observe a few guidelines. Identifying what you can get done and engaging others to help you are key factors in delegating properly. In this chapter, you learned how to determine what you do best while identifying others who find joy in what you might not. Delegation does not mean you dump undesirable tasks on others, but you empower them to do what you might not have time to accomplish yourself. Because delegation is based on trust and confidence in others, we established a trust test to ensure that your delegates are the best choice. You learned how to farm out guilt-free and to empower others without micromanaging them. Mentoring while monitoring is an effective tool in delegation. You learned how not to point fingers and to know when it is best *not* to delegate. The balance between autonomy and control is a fine one, and you know you cannot expect others to complete the job exactly as you would. Finally, we discussed loyalty-building measures that include public acknowledgment and celebration.

As you build on all the principles you have learned, you will discover that the final principle we will discuss in the next chapter flows through all one hundred of the others. Incidentally, it turns out to be the most basic principle of all.

11

Just One Thing:
Final Way to Save Time

I KNOW I'M ALWAYS SUPPOSED TO LISTEN TO
MYSELF, BUT WHICH "SELF"?

> Time is how we live it, not what's measured by the clock.
>
> —Zoketsu Norman Fischer[1]

Congratulations! You have made it this far. Your personal bank account of time has been reclaimed as you realize how simple the principles behind the power of slow truly are. The final principle for rescuing your relationship with time boils down to a single word: choice.

Decision making is not something we innately know how to

do. Other than the fight or flight instinct, we are not imbued with a generic sense of nuanced choice from birth. Like so many of the other principles we have addressed in this book, making choices is a skill set you can hone over time. The first thing you need to know is that you have a choice. We all do.

You can choose to view time as a lacking resource, a petulant cousin of death, or an enormous ally that works with you at every turn. You can choose to view your life as dark or light, fast or slow. You have enormous power to hand-select how you see things.

The power of choice became apparent to me at an ice cream parlor one day. Standing in front of the counter with my then three-year-old daughter, we stared at the rainbow-swirled selection with watery mouths. My daughter stood there, sucking her finger, unable to decide which ice cream she should take. It was information overload at its best. To narrow her choices, I pointed to two separate tubs of ice cream. "Chocolate or vanilla?" I asked with a tinge of impatience in my voice. I was in a hurry. It was well before the power of slow had even crossed my mind, much less entered my life. I was a busy, busy person with many, many things to do. Why couldn't she choose? I could almost hear the ticking from the clock tower outside the window. Like so many Americans, my schedule could be likened to that of a high-profile doctor's office. Without asking her again, I ordered her vanilla with chocolate sprinkles. It seemed like a reasonable compromise. After all, I had to get going. I had *things to do.*

As my daughter licked her quickly melting ice cream in the shopping center parking lot, I wondered when I had become so harried. What was I rushing toward? It was a dreamy midsummer afternoon. A nearby water fountain hosted a gaggle of children splashing themselves silly. Despite the idyllic scene, I felt time pressing against my temples in a viselike grip.

Little did I know in that moment that I had a choice about how I spent my time. I had bought into a paradigm that dictated my schedule. It clearly didn't work for me, and despite my daughter's immediate gratitude for any ice cream at all, it probably wouldn't work for her or her generation either. I had become so addicted to speed that I had no regard for slowness, or, heaven forbid, mindfulness. A piercing feeling of emptiness that I was clearly missing the very thing I should want the most nearly paralyzed me. In that moment, I made my first step toward freedom. Instead of rushing to the car, I sat down with my daughter on a neighboring bench. We chased a few pigeons and raised our faces to the sun. For a moment in time, I had suspended my disbelief about time as friend. Walking at my daughter's pace, I gently guided her back to the car and drove the speed limit. By the time I got home, slow was already beginning to feel pretty good.

The more I thought about it over the following years, the more I began to wonder if there could be another way to live beyond the time lines and deadlines in which we have become entangled. Could we embrace a slower way of life without turning back the clock? Does slow mean backwards? Wrong? Stupid? Certainly not.

Throughout this book, we have addressed one hundred ways to live the power of slow. While some may have been obvious, others might have surprised you. Perhaps you were amazed that when you tried one or two of the exercises your thinking began to shift without your even trying. In this chapter, I'd like to weave all the ideas together by illuminating them through the framework of choice. No one else has the privilege of living your life but you. As we mentioned in the very beginning, our lives are encased between two time notations—time of birth and time of death. The average American lives 78.14 years. In between, we have an average of 28,521 days or approximately 684,504 hours translated into 41,070,240 minutes to be within the confines of this thing called time. While it may be unrealistic to expect ourselves to experience ecstasy every moment of every day, you can choose your attitude about everything. Nelson Mandela spent thirty-two years in prison. He made a choice that impacted millions. You also have the power to make choices that leave you empowered, emboldened, and unbounded by time or place.

Choice requires consciousness. It requires a deep-seated awareness about yourself. Maybe you are at the beginning of your self-awareness journey. Perhaps you have been exploring who you are for a very long time. Either way you need to remember that you always have a choice. Like time itself, you can use choice to your advantage.

Judith Wright dedicates her entire book *The One Decision* to the one commitment you decide for yourself in life. She offers her readers a life of *more* through the one individualized choice we make at the book's outset. While it may be simplified thinking that one thing could make all the difference, it holds true that choice is the basis of everything. Couple your commitment with a solid relationship with time, and you are truly unstoppable.

When you choose to view time as money, you choose to limit yourself completely. You internally trade your personal bank account of time, making it a scarce commodity in a system dictated by supply and demand. The less you have of it, the more you want it. The more you want it, the more stressed you become. You recognize there are limitations, yet you live at a pace that attempts to beat the speed of light. Because we are made up of light, we are trying to go faster than ourselves. Imagine what would happen if we traveled faster than light. Would we disappear?

We can choose to shift our collective dialogue about time as a lacking resource to a more powerful view of time as friend. The first step is divorcing time from money and attaching it to a more personal relationship each person can enjoy. We can choose a value shift toward what "time well spent" really means. When we embrace time in a different way, we can move more readily into a more dreamlike state of flow when we are working, playing, or interacting with others.

Time as friend also means the death of multitasking. It is a myth at best, and our continuous attempt to juggle too many things at once leaves us war weary as we realize the futility of clock combat. Technology has allowed us unprecedented opportunities for speed and efficiency, but at what cost? We expect ourselves and others to accomplish more in less time while sacrificing the quality of our exchange. We allow gadgets that ring, ping, and sing to interrupt our daily flow. If you have ever panicked because you forgot to charge your cell phone battery, you will see how much you rely on gadgets as you go about your daily business.

We can choose to take back our family meals in digital-free zones. We can revive the art of conversation by speaking in full sentences with one another while sustaining eye contact. It may sound radical, but banning devices from the dinner table will improve your quality of life as you begin to concentrate on the food you eat and the people around you. We can use technology to our advantage by taking the phone off the hook, removing the television from our main living space, and reclaiming our relationships. Balancing our commitments with our resources, we can choose to spend our time on the things and people we love.

Our habits must be in alignment with our commitment to the power of slow. Without good habits to reinforce the principles, the power of slow just remains a really good, but unexecuted, idea. Taking inventory of the habits that support a good relationship with time is an essential step. We can choose to replace poor habits with empowered ones. Identifying our pain points can help us harness the willingness to alter our patterns. In a moment of "I can't take it anymore," we can utilize that energy toward positive change. Sometimes it is simply a matter of giving yourself a break to evaluate what works for you and what does not.

You cannot walk into a building unless there is a door. Creating the opening for positive change is an important step in forming new habits. Sometimes it is as simple as choosing a different route to get to work that breathes new life into your routine. As you enter new spaces, you begin to see the world with a different set of eyes.

We have identified the time-robbing characteristics of being a "yes-man." It is here that choice plays a starring role. When we identify why we tend to agree to things we would rather not do, we are closer to finding ways to make a different choice. Sometimes we think it will be easier to agree to something than to "fight the fight," but the reality is we teach people how to treat us. Saying yes now will only make saying no harder the next time. We need to set limits for ourselves and others by declining to engage in things that do not serve our higher purpose. Keeping our word is an integral part of living a life of integrity. If we agree to something to which we later do not show up, it is often worse than saying no in the first place.

Procrastination is a weak form of saying no, but it is most often saying no to ourselves. We put things off in the hopes of avoiding a painful experience. All the while we draw it out by spending more time and energy on avoiding the task than on that which the task itself would require. We can choose to recognize our ability to command our own ship, creating pockets of win that reward us for moving forward when we would rather not. We have learned to tackle hard things earlier in our day to free up our minds for more enjoyable tasks later on. Communication plays a key role in clearing up any misunderstandings that might lead to avoidant behavior. We can choose to tackle issues head-on or allow them to fester, thereby giving them fodder to feed off our time and energy reserves. Filing taxes on time is a prime example of making the choice to slay the *Schweinehund* (pig-dog) that holds us back from living the life we deserve.

After all this hard work of avoiding procrastination, we start to realize the benefits of taking time off. We can choose to look at leisure activities as a purposeful way to spend our time. Listing what we love to do in our free time helps us become aware of what we truly value. We can test out what it is like to take time off by slowly disengaging ourselves from the immediacy that informs our lives. Creating open-ended events to which your friends are invited to come and go as they please will help spread the power of slow by sheer association. We can choose to reclaim the art of hanging out by eking out a few moments each day to enjoy a moment of nothingness. On those days when we need to carve out more time, we can take a full day off to smell the roses by visiting the great outdoors or attending a personal interest seminar.

Even when we cannot take time off for days on end, we can integrate more time-outs during our day. Developing an exercise group at work or taking a quick nap can help you sustain your energy, making you more efficient at work. Simulating sleep through a simple finger-lifting or yogic-breathing exercise can be equally beneficial. We can choose to honor the space between things, called *ma* in Japanese, by actively seeking out pockets of respite each day. We can influence our surroundings through smell, sound, and color.

While we might not be able to control other people, we can certainly control our own reactions to them. Managing expectations well can save you mountains of time. We have seen that identifying which expectations exist is a crucial first step to managing them. By surprising people with the underpromise-overdeliver model, we can effect positive relations with others. We can choose to communicate effectively by speaking the same language as our counterparts and defining what we mean when we use words such as "now" and "later."

Eliminating distractions can also help us improve our relationship with time. It is based on the priorities we have and the purpose we choose. When we know what our commitment is, we can more readily devise ways to focus on that goal. It is important to choose a plan that works for you by specifying what your focus will be. Identifying stumbling blocks that make you lose focus, then avoiding them, is crucial. The underlying principle of self-forgiveness implies choice: You can choose to be all things to all people or forgive yourself for your limitations. Sometimes we need to create a sacred space to keep our eyes on the prize. We can choose to remove ourselves from chaos by making room for our own creativity. We need to differentiate between what it important, urgent, or merely a distraction. It is often based on our own choice.

Thinking time is undervalued in our society, yet it is an equally important part of the creative process. Every one of us is a creative human being with his or her own uniqueness. Honoring the time it takes to get to the moment of creation is also based on the choices we make. We either choose to allow our subconscious mind to work for us, or we crowd it out with only conscious-driven thoughts that often only skim the surface of our potential. Self-reflection contributes to human progress. Without it, we would be merely marking time and never truly enjoying it. Self-care through exercise and meditation is also a personal choice. How you choose to care for yourself will impact the quality, and to some extent, the length of your life. Self-care and caring for others contribute to longevity.

Finally, we come to the choice of doing things ourselves or asking others for help. Delegating tasks that contribute to others' personal and professional growth is a skill like any other. Based on trust, delegation is a powerful tool in living the power of slow as you realize we do not live in a vacuum but in fellowship with others. Empowering people to be the best they can be helps you become the best you can be. As we have learned, blame and micromanaging have no part in delegation. It is your choice whether you wish to trust others or not, but trust is the foundation of our relationship with time. As you consider the balance between autonomy and control, you begin to realize every action we take in life is based on a decision we alone make. While we live in communion with humanity, we sometimes act as if we are all alone. It is the paradox of life that we all possess our own time while sharing it with others. Take time to celebrate the wins in your life. Light or dark. Fast or slow. Chocolate or vanilla. You choose.

The power of slow is a simple, if not always easy, road. It raises us up to our highest potential; the great news is we can share this principle with others to create a network of support as we take this journey together. If we see our friends sliding into a time-starved panic, we can remind them of what is truly important. Let us embrace the dance for as long as the music plays. Then, as we make withdrawals from our personal bank account of time, we will know we have done the very best we can.

After all, time, and the way we choose to live it, is all there really is.

Epilogue
"Busy" Is a Four-Letter Word

My brain was sizzling from another grueling fourteen-hour day. Before closing shop for the night, I dashed off an e-mail to my oldest sister about how tired I felt. I had worked so hard for so many years, yet nothing I had worked for seemed to have panned out as planned. Within minutes I received a response that would change my world forever. She acknowledged my persistence and dedication, yet she cautioned me that overworking wouldn't lead me down the Yellow Brick Road. In fact, it is counterproductive, she reasoned. It only serves to wear your spirit thin. A joyless, threadbare spirit serves no one. "'Busy,'" she wrote, "is a four-letter word." It took me a full minute before I blinked. Her poetic leanings had always inspired me, yet those few words hid immeasurable poignancy.

In that moment, I realized busy does not equal life. Busy is activity. And purposeless activity is pointless.

I took a long, hard look at my own activity level. How much of it was really serving my higher purpose? More important, did I even know what my higher purpose was? I thought so, but as I began to evaluate what I did compared to what I wanted to do, I saw a discrepancy so large that I nearly grew red with shame. I began to believe there were more people like me who worked too much, spent too much time doing things they did not enjoy, and had a negative relationship to the clock. Time starvation is a collective issue, exacerbated by technological advances that ping, whir, and buzz at us. While I have always been a proponent of the Internet and its digital offshoots, I also began to see the downside to instant availability. The blur between public and private has made our existence fuzzy. We are on call to what we feel are universal forces beyond our control. The good news is we are wrong.

Throughout this book I have selected positive case studies of people learning they have more control than they ever realized. Their admirable lives offer proof that powerful living does not take much, but it does take something: commitment. Embracing the power of slow requires a willingness to adopt a saner pace of life that does not involve the knee-jerk response of being so busy. In effect, telling someone you are busy is like telling them to bug off. Busyness is indeed a state of mind that leaves no room for mindfulness. It is not an act, but a mind-set. So is the power of slow.

During the course of my research, I traveled near and far in search of people's understanding of time. I asked hundreds of people from around the world about their belief system and how busy or not busy they felt. Some, like the Indian yogi Bikram Choudhury, the founder of hot yoga who travels the world and purportedly works twenty-four hours a day, told me after a torturous three-hour workout in Munich that time is God. Others reiterated Benjamin Franklin's belief that time is money. Others still responded that time is a precious commodity. No matter the response, everyone had a personal interpretation of what time means to them.

Regardless of religion, country, or creed, time remains the only thing we truly have in common. Truth be told, time is what connects us all. May your life be enriched by the power of slow as you spend the time you have resting squarely in *your* hands.

Notes

Introduction

1. Tolle, *The Power of Now.*
2. Robinson and Godbey, *Time for Life*, 34.
3. Fraser, *Time, the Familiar Stranger*, 43.

1: Time Is Money . . . and Other Lies

1. Franklin, "Advice to a Young Tradesman," in Weems, *The Life of Benjamin Franklin*, 226. Italics in the original.
2. Robinson and Godbey, *Time for Life*, 25. Originally quoted in E. Graham and C. Crossan, "Too Much to Do, Too Little Time," *Wall Street Journal*, March 8, 1996.
3. Canfield and Switzer, *The Success Principles.*
4. See also Stefan Klein, "Time Out of Mind," *New York Times*, March 7, 2008.
5. "There is nothing either good or bad, but thinking makes it so." (*Hamlet* Act 2, Scene II).
6. Csikszentmihalyi, *Flow.*
7. www.LightHeartedMedicine.com.

2: The Myth of Multitasking

1. Lohr, "Slow Down, Brave Multitasker, and Don't Read This in Traffic."
2. Hamilton, "'Internal Chatter' Limits Multitasking As People Age."
3. Poldrack et al., "Multi-tasking Adversely Affects Brain's Learning."
4. Harrison, "Verizon Works to Let Other Devices on Network."
5. U.S. Department of Transportation, *The Impact of Driver Inattention On Near-Crash/Crash Risk.*
6. Francis and Birch, "Does Eating During Television Viewing Affect Preschool Children's Intake?"
7. For an example of his work, see Abercrombie, "A Phonetician's View of Verse Structure," and Abercrombie, *Elements of General Phonetics.*

3: Creatures of Habit

1. www.SlowDownFast.com.

4: Power of Slow—Just Say No!

1. http://about.skype.com/2009/02/allnew_skype_now_available.html (accessed February 15, 2009).

5: Procrastination Station

1. Reprinted with permission from Global Knowledge. Originally published in Egan, "Delegate or Suffocate."
2. Associated Press, January 12, 2007, as seen in http://www.sptimes.com/2007/01/12/Worldandnation/Five_year_procrastina.shtml.
3. Steel and König, "Integrating Theories of Motivation."
4. Faiza Elmasry, *Procrastinating Nothing New, But Getting Worse,* Elmasry Report, Voice of America, January 27, 2007. http://www.voanews.com/english/archive/2007–01/2007–01–26-voa70.cfm (accessed November 22, 2008).

5.   http://blogs.psychologytoday.com/blog/don039t-delay/200807/
     living-well-dying-well-some-reflections-regret-grief-and-procrasti
     nation.
6.   Reprint from *Daily Health News,* "Zander on Overcoming Excuses
     That Hold You Back."
7.   Archer et al., "A Length Polymorphism."
8.   *Businesswire,* April 2, 2007. http://www.thefreelibrary.com/_/print/
     PrintArticle.aspx?id=161384742.
9.   Steel, "The Nature of Procrastination."

6: Free Time Is Not Expensive. It's, Well, Free!

1.   *The Last Lecture,* 111.
2.   Quoted in Gibbs, "How America Has Run Out of Time."
3.   Leisure Trends Group, http://www.leisuretrends.com/ShowArticle
     .aspx?ID=301&EID=111&sid=WW8SRYSQWJOPIAFIOGRCE (accessed
     September 10, 2008).
4.   Urban Parks Master Plan Leisure and Recreation Trends Analysis,
     Edmonton Community Services, October 2002, 46. http://www
     .edmonton.ca/CityGov/CommServices/LeisureAndRecreationTrends-
     AnalysisForUrbanParks.pdf.
5.   Robinson and Martin, "What Do Happy People Do?"
6.   Levine, *A Geography of Time,* 94.
7.   Findings reported at biannual meeting of "Work, Stress and Health"
     in Miami, Florida, in 2007, an event sponsored by the American Psy-
     chological Association. As viewed here: http://www.aftau.org/site/
     News2?page=NewsArticle&id=6009.
8.   Stoops, "Educational Attainment in the United States: 2003."

7: Time-Outs

1.   CIA World Factbook (2008). This number includes the unemployed.
     https://www.cia.gov/library/publications/the-world-factbook/geos/
     us.html#Econ (accessed September 11, 2008).
2.   U.S. Department of Labor, *American Time Use Survey—2007 Re-
     sults.*

3. Gibbs, "How America Has Run Out of Time."
4. Weiss, "Americans May Be Getting Enough Sleep After All, Report Says."
5. Zimbardo, et al., "Liberating Behavior from Time-Bound Control."
6. Quoted in *Science Daily*, November 5, 2007. http://www.sciencedaily.com/releases/2007/11/071101085021.htm (accessed September 9, 2008).
7. USDA's *Amber Waves* newsletter, June 2008. http://www.ers.usda.gov/AmberWaves/June08/DataFeature (accessed September 17, 2008).
8. Mancino and Kinsey, "Is Dietary Knowledge Enough?"
9. http://www.therapytimes.com/content=0402J84C489EAC8440A040441 (accessed October 8, 2008).

8: Expectation Management

1. Vaidya, "Four Quadrant Expectation Management."

9: Focus Factor

1. Copyright 2008 Ralph S. Marston, Jr. Used by permission. Originally published in "The Daily Motivator" at www.dailymotivator.com.
2. http://www.wired.com/techbiz/media/magazine/15–09/st_pechakucha.
3. Jackson, *Distracted*.
4. http://www.theatlantic.com/doc/200807/google.
5. Burns et al., "Cardiorespiratory Fitness and Brain Atrophy in Early Alzheimer Disease."
6. Davidson et al., "Alterations in Brain and Immune Function Produced by Mindfulness Meditation."

10: Delegation

1. Egan, "Delegate or Suffocate."
2. Eikenberry, "The Dangers of Delegation."
3. Post and Neimark, *Why Good Things Happen to Good People*.

4. "Bosses: Killing Them with Kindness Pays Off," *The Globe and Mail*, October 8, 2008. http://www.theglobeandmail.com/servlet/story/ LAC.20081008.CABRIEF08–1/TPStory/Business (accessed October 8, 2008).

11: Just One Thing

1. Fischer, "Simple Yet Astounding Ways to Calm Down."

Helpful Web Sites

www.bls.gov/tus
www.Deadcellzones.com
www.LightHeartedMedicine.com
www.paceoflife.co.uk
www.PeterPamelaRose.com
www.PowerofSlow.org
www.SlowDownFast.com
www.SlowFood.com
www.SlowPlanet.com
www.TherapyTimes.com
www.yumyumdish.com

Bibliography

Abercrombie, David. "A Phonetician's View of Verse Structure." *Linguistics* 6, (1964): 5–13.

Abercrombie, David. *Elements of General Phonetics*. Edinburgh: Edinburgh University Press, 1967.

Albom, Mitch. *Tuesdays with Morrie: An Old Man, a Young Man, and Life's Greatest Lesson*. New York: Broadway Books, 2002.

Archer, Simon N., et al. "A Length Polymorphism in the Circadian Clock Gene Per3 Is Linked to Delayed Sleep Phase Syndrome and Extreme Diurnal Preference." *SLEEP* 26, no. 4 (2003): 413–15.

Burns, J. M., et al. "Cardiorespiratory Fitness and Brain Atrophy in Early Alzheimer Disease." *Neurology Online* 71 (2008): 210–16. http://www.neurology.org/cgi/content/abstract/71/3/210 (accessed August 2, 2008).

Cameron, Julia. *The Artist's Way: A Spiritual Path to Higher Creativity*. New York: G. P. Putnam's Sons, 1992.

Canfield, Jack, with Janet Switzer. *The Success Principles: How to Get from Where You Are to Where You Want to Be*. New York: HarperCollins Publishers, 2005.

Connor, Bobbi. *Unplugged Play*. New York: Workman Publishing, 2007.

Covey, Stephen. *7 Habits of Highly Effective People*. New York: Free Press, 2004.

Croteau, David, and William Hoynes. *Media/Society: Industries, Images, and Audiences*. Thousand Oaks: Pine Forge Press, 1997.

Csikszentmihalyi, Mihaly. *Flow: The Psychology of Optimal Experience*. New York: HarperPerennial Modern Classics, 2008.

Davidson, Richard J., et al. "Alterations in Brain and Immune Function Produced by Mindfulness Meditation." *Psychosomatic Medicine* 65 (2003): 564–70.

Egan, Brian Denis. "Delegate or Suffocate—The Art of Working Through Others." *Global Knowledge Expert Reference Series of White Papers*. www.globalknowledge.com, 2005.

Eikenberry, Kevin. "The Dangers of Delegation." *EyesOnSales.com*, September 15, 2008. http://eyesonsales.com/archives/blog/the_dangers_of_delegation (accessed October 8, 2008).

Ellis, Albert, and William Knaus. *Overcoming Procrastination*. New York: Signet Books, 1979.

Emoto, Masaru. *The Hidden Messages in Water*. Translated by David Thayne. Hillsboro: Beyond Words Publishing, 2004.

Ferriss, Timothy. *The 4-Hour Workweek: Escape 9-5, Live Anywhere, and Join the New Rich*. New York: Crown Publishing, 2007.

Fiore, Neil. *The Now Habit: A Strategic Program for Overcoming Procrastination and Enjoying Guilt-Free Play*. London: Penguin Books, 2007.

Fischer, Norman. "Simple Yet Astounding Ways to Calm Down." *O, The Oprah Magazine*, September 2008. http://www.oprah.com/article/omagazine/200809_omag_busy.

Francis, Lori, and Leah Birch. "Does Eating During Television Viewing Affect Preschool Children's Intake?" *Journal of the American Dietetic Association* 106, no. 4 (April 2006): 598–600.

Franklin, Benjamin. "Advice to a Young Tradesman," 1748, in Benjamin Franklin, Mason Locke Weems. *The Life of Benjamin Franklin*. Published by M. Carey, 1817. Original from Harvard University. Digitized version from December 5, 2007.

Fraser, J. T. *Time, the Familiar Stranger*. Amherst: University of Massachusetts Press, 1987.

Gibbs, Nancy. "How America Has Run Out of Time." *Time*, April 24, 1989, 58–67.

Graham, E., and C. Crossan. "Too Much to Do, Too Little Time." *Wall Street Journal*, March 8, 1996.

Hamilton, Jon. "'Internal Chatter' Limits Multitasking As People Age." *Morning Edition*, National Public Radio, October 30, 2008.

Harrison, Crayton. "Verizon Works to Let Other Devices on Network." *Washington Post*, March 20, 2008.

Honoré, Carl. *In Praise of Slow: How a Worldwide Movement Is Challenging the Cult of Speed.* London: Orion, 2005.

Hunnicutt, Benjamin. *Kellogg's Six-Hour Day.* Philadelphia: Temple University Press, 1996.

Jackson, Maggie. *Distracted: The Erosion of Attention and the Coming Dark Age.* New York: Prometheus Books, 2008.

Jönsson, Bodil. *Unwinding the Clock: Ten Thoughts on Our Relationship to Time.* Translated by Tina Nunnally. Orlando: Harcourt, 2001.

Klein, Stefan. "Time Out of Mind." *New York Times*, March 7, 2008. http://www.nytimes.com/2008/03/07/opinion/07klein.html (accessed October 21, 2008).

Klein, Stefan, and Shelley Frisch. *The Secret Pulse of Time: Making Sense of Life's Scarcest Commodity.* New York: Da Capo Press, 2007.

Levine, Robert. *A Geography of Time: The Temporal Misadventures of a Social Psychologist or How Every Culture Keeps Time Just a Little Bit Differently.* Oxford: Oneworld Publications, 2006.

Lohr, Steven. "Slow Down, Brave Multitasker, and Don't Read This in Traffic." *New York Times*, March 25, 2007. http://www.nytimes.com/2007/03/25/business/25multi.html?partner=permalink&exprod=permalink (accessed October 28, 2008).

Maltz, Maxwell. *Psycho-Cybernetics.* New York: Pocket Books, 1969.

Mancino, Lisa, and Jean Kinsey. "Is Dietary Knowledge Enough? Hunger, Stress, and Other Roadblocks to Healthy Eating." *Economic Research Report*, August 2008. http://www.ers.usda.gov/Publications/ERR62 (accessed October 29, 2008).

Michon, John A. "J. T. Fraser's 'Levels of Temporality' as Cognitive Representations." In *Time, Science, and Society in China and the West (The Study of Time V)*, edited by J. T. Fraser and N. Lawrence, 51–66. Amherst, MA: University of Massachusetts Press, 1986.

Pausch, Randy, with Jeffrey Zaslow. *The Last Lecture.* New York: Hyperion, 2008.

Poldrack, Russell, et al. "Multi-tasking Adversely Affects Brain's Learning." In *UCLA Psychologists Report.* Los Angeles: University of California, 2006.

Post, Stephen, and Jill Neimark. *Why Good Things Happen to Good People.* New York: Broadway Books, 2007.

Rifkin, Jeremy. *Time Wars: The Primary Conflict in Human History*. New York: Simon & Schuster, 1989.

Robinson, John P., and Geoffrey Godbey. *Time for Life: The Surprising Ways Americans Use Their Time*. University Park: Pennsylvania State University Press, 1997.

Robinson, John P., and Steven Martin. "What Do Happy People Do?" *Social Indicators Research* 89 (July 31, 2008): 565–71.

Savage, Elayne. *Breathing Room—Creating Space to Be a Couple*. Oakland, MA: New Harbinger Publications, 2001.

Seligman, Martin. *Authentic Happiness: Using the New Positive Psychology to Realize Your Potential for Lasting Fulfillment*. New York: Free Press, 2002.

Steel, Piers. "The Nature of Procrastination: A Meta-Analytic and Theoretical Review of Quintessential Self-Regulatory Failure." *Psychological Bulletin* 133, no. 1 (2007): 65–94.

Steel, Piers, and Cornelius König. "Integrating Theories of Motivation." *Academy of Management Review* 31, no. 4 (2006): 899–913.

Stoops, Nicole. "Educational Attainment in the United States: 2003." Current Population Reports, June 2004. Washington, D.C.: U.S. Census Bureau. http://www.census.gov/prod/2004pubs/p20-550.pdf (accessed September 25, 2008).

Tolle, Eckhart. *The Power of Now: A Guide to Spiritual Enlightenment*. Novato: New World Library, 2004.

U.S. Department of Labor. *American Time Use Survey—2007 Results*. Washington, D.C.: Bureau of Labor Statistics, 2008. www.bls.gov/tus.

U.S. Department of Transportation. *The Impact of Driver Inattention On Near-Crash/Crash Risk: An Analysis Using the 100-Car Naturalistic Driving Study Data*. April 2006. http://www.noys.org/Driver%20Inattention %20Report.pdf (accessed November 9, 2008).

Vaidya, Kirti. "Four Quadrant Expectation Management." *DeveloperWorks*, May 15, 2005. http://www.ibm.com/developerworks/rational/library/ may05/vaidya/index.html.

Weiss, Rick. "Americans May Be Getting Enough Sleep After All, Report Says." *Washington Post*, March 12, 2008.

Wiseman, Richard. *Quirkology: The Curious Science of Everyday Lives*. Oxford: Pan Macmillan, 2008.

Wright, Judith. *The One Decision: Make the Single Choice That Will Lead to a Life of More.* New York: Tarcher/Penguin, 2007.

Zander, Lauren. "Zander on Overcoming Excuses That Hold You Back. Simple Realization Provides New-Found Freedom." *Daily Health News,* January 15, 2008. http://www.bottomlinesecrets.com/blpnet/article .html?article_id=44048.

Zimbardo, Philip G, et al. "Liberating Behavior from Time-Bound Control: Expanding the Present Through Hypnosis." *Journal of Applied Social Psychology* 1, no. 4 (1971): 305–23.